THE COMMUNION OF SAINTS

A Study of the Origin and Development of Luther's Doctrine of the Church

THE COMMUNION OF SAINTS

A Study of the Origin and Development of Luther's Doctrine of the Church

by

HERMAN AMBERG PREUS, M.Th., Ph.D.

Professor of New Testament Exegesis and Symbolics
Luther Theological Seminary
St. Paul, Minnesota

WIPF & STOCK · Eugene, Oregon

Wipf and Stock Publishers
199 W 8th Ave, Suite 3
Eugene, OR 97401

The Communion of Saints
A Study of the Origin and Development of Luther's Doctrine of the Church
By Preus, Herman Amberg
ISBN 13: 978-1-60608-309-3
Publication date 12/04/2008
Previously published by Augsburg Press, 1948

TO THE GLORY OF GOD
IN THE
BODY OF CHRIST

CONTENTS

PART ONE
LUTHER AND THE DOCTRINE OF THE CHURCH IN HISTORY

Chapter One
Luther and the Problem of the Church 3

Chapter Two
Luther and the Ancient Tradition 11
  Back to the Scriptures
  Traditions versus *The Tradition*
  The Tradition from St. Paul to Luther

PART TWO
LUTHER THE ROMAN CATHOLIC

Chapter Three
Luther the Obedient Son 37
  His Early Environment and the Doctrine of the Church
  First Stages in the Development of the Doctrine

Chapter Four
Luther the Catholic Critic 42
  Lectures on the Psalms
  Lectures on Romans

Chapter Five
Luther the Rebel 57
  The Indulgence Controversy
  The Leipzig Disputation

PART THREE
LUTHER THE REFORMER

Chapter Six
  The Communion of Saints 75
Chapter Seven
  The Object of Our Faith 84
Chapter Eight
  The Perennial Reformation 95
Chapter Nine
  The Experience of Holy Communion 110
Chapter Ten
  The Keys of the Kingdom 128

ABBREVIATIONS

The following abbreviations have been used throughout this work in referring to the various editions of Luther's works:

W.—D. Martin Luther's Werke. Kritische Gesammtausgabe. Weimar, H. Böhlau, 1883-

Holman—Works of Martin Luther . . . Philadelphia, Pa., A. J. Holman Co., 1915-32.

Op. var. arg.—D. Martini Lutheri Opera latina varii argumenti ad reformationis historiam imprimis pertinentia. Curavit dr. Henricus Schmidt . . . Frankofurti et Erlangae, Heyder et Zimmer, 1865-73.

Walch—D. Martin Luthers . . . Sämmtliche Schriften . . . hrsg. von Johann Georg Walch . . . Halle, J. J. Gebauer, 1740-53.

Erlangen—Dr. Martin Luther's Sämmtliche Werke . . . Erlangen, Carl Heyder, 1826-57.

Lenker—The Precious and Sacred Writings of Martin Luther . . . edited by John Nicholas Lenker. Minneapolis, Minn., Lutherans in all Lands Co., 1903-

The frequent references to Luther's *Dictata super Psalterium* have been abbreviated by using "Ps." plus the number of the Psalm, followed by the reference to the Weimar edition of his works.

Part One

LUTHER AND THE DOCTRINE OF THE CHURCH IN HISTORY

CHAPTER ONE

Luther AND THE PROBLEM OF THE CHURCH

"Protestantism has no church, in the full Christian sense." Either that is a rank libel that demands an answer from Protestantism, or it is a fact that compels us to do something about it. The man who said it[1] is himself, like Harnack who said it before him, a Protestant. And as if to chide his faltering Church he continues, "Not only so, but the spirit of Protestantism is afraid of the church, afraid to be a church. It has recoiled so far and so intensely from the Roman conception of the Church that it is unable to envisage any realization of the Church Catholic which is not Roman."

If we are thinking in terms of Protestantism as a whole, we shall find it difficult to answer that charge. Look at the Edinburgh Conference of 1937, how it wrestled with the doctrine of the Church! The Report, with its frank statement of divergent opinions on this doctrine, is a partial, but hardly an adequate, answer to the charge that "Protestantism has no church."

In so far as Protestantism has preserved its catholicity and sense of continuity with the Church of the centuries it has an adequate doctrine of the Church, defined by

---
[1]Editorial in *The Christian Century*, LV (Nov. 2, 1938) 1321

Luther himself on the basis of the Scriptures. In so far as it has yielded to sectarianism, it "has no church."

This uncomfortable situation in which Protestantism finds itself, compels it to recover for itself the doctrine of the Church, and with it that priceless possession, a consciousness of the holy, Christian Church, the Communion of Saints, the Body of Christ. Pity the poor sectarian individualist who does not know the comfort of the Church, the "glory of the communion of saints," as Luther refers to it!

For the sake of that scattered army of Christian "lone wolves" in the world, the rediscovery of the Scriptural doctrine of the Church is important. For the sake of saving Protestantism from the disintegrating ravages of sectarianism, it must be reiterated that there is one holy Church. For the sake of a Protestantism which has been flirting with deviating tendencies till its fingers are dripping with sentimental subjectivism in life and worship, we must confront it with the reality of the Church and the riches of its inheritance.

Some folks see something sinister in this kind of language. Is it not a first step back into that deadly Roman ecclesiasticism from which the Reformation once set us free? Four hundred years of history would rather indicate that the Lutheran Church, with the whole of Protestantism, has as much to fear from sectarian individualism and rattle-brained subjectivism as it has from Romanism. And when I say this I say it with due regard and gratitude for the spiritual quickening that sound piety and evangelistic fervor in many quarters have brought to the Lutheran Church in our own day. Apart from this, however, we have been witnessing something of that unbalanced emotional "Schwärmerei," which brought Luther headlong out of the Wartburg to halt the destruction of the Church as Church. It is quite possible that Luther would again "burst out of Wartburg" if he saw the way history is repeating itself in some quarters of his Church. Lutheran hymns gone with the wind in favor of jolly jingles, liturgy and worship desiccated by clerical individualists, confessional theology giving way to a sectarian "Biblicism" which some are calling the "sweet Jesus theology."

Is it too far-fetched to tie these things up with the fact that we have lost the sense of the Church? We have taken the Reformation principle of individual liberty and carried it to the extremes of license. Have we forgotten, perhaps, that there is a holy Christian Church in which we believe? Or do we not believe in it any more?

If the idea of the Church has become to us a lifeless theory for theologians to debate, we need a lesson from the suffering churches of Europe and Asia. The cries of persecuted millions have been ringing in our ears ever since the Russian Revolution. It was a cry to the Church from Christians who had learned by bitter experience the wonderful reality of the Communion of Saints. "Whether one member suffer, all the members suffer with it." But how shall we account for the apathy of the American Church to that agonizing cry? Does not the answer lie in our narrow denominational unconsciousness of the greater fact of the Communion of Saints? Proud and satisfied with our Americanized Church, which had at last cut loose from our foreign mother's apron strings, we became oblivious and calloused to the sufferings of other members of the body of Christ, forgetting that we were by the grace of God members of His Body. We had become unworthy successors of the great Reformer who said, "To no one is any grace given only for himself, but for the benefit of the Church."[2]

But then happily things began to change. A wave of Luther research swept the European continent, starting in Germany. And as the true Luther emerged, a revitalized Lutheran theology began to appear. Men were driven back to the Word of God. The accretions picked up in the successive movements of dead orthodoxy, subjective pietism, and rationalism, were thrown off, one at a time. The paralyzing influence of the Prussian Union became unbearable. Then the Lutheran theologians threw themselves into an intensive study of the doctrine of the Church. The persecution of Hitler and Rosenberg and Goebbels spurred them on in this study. Now it was no longer a can of dry theology to be opened in the theologian's study and subjected to microscopic examination. Now it was a matter of life and death for every Christian in Germany. Literature began to pour off the press, probing deeply into the doctrine of the Church. Out of that strife there came to those Christians again the comforting consciousness of the Communion of Saints. Their outward intercourse with Christendom cut off by the laws of extreme nationalism, they reached out in faith and in prayer to clasp hands in spirit with the saints of all lands and to confess anew, *"Credo in sanctam ecclesiam catholicam; sanctorum communionem."*

Like the cry out of Russia came the cry of German Christians longing for the comfort of the Communion of Saints. With the fighting voices of the Niemöllers came the steadying voices of other leaders in the suffering Church. Men like Bishop Lilje call on fellow-Christians to be strong in faith. Let them consider the trials of

---
[2] Ps. 112. W. IV, 256, L. 35.

the Church of the Reformation in the days of Luther. In a great speech delivered in Hannover in August, 1935, he reminds them that "the Reformers bore up under the battle, because they were not so short-sighted as to think that the Church would cease to exist tomorrow. They clung to the word of their Confession, '*quod una sancta ecclesia perpetuo mansura sit*,' 'that the one holy Church is to continue forever.' Human institutions could be condemned to death by the storms of revolution sweeping over them. But of the work of God, we confess that it abides; 'Thy work can no man hinder, thy labor must not rest.' That applies also to the Church."[3]

Under the pressure of suffering, the glorious consciousness of the Communion of Saints began to spread across the Continent, through Scandinavia, and across the sea to America. The Lutheran churches were finally becoming aware that there is a Lutheran Church of the world, and that far beyond that there is *one* holy Christian Church, the Communion of Saints.

This resurgence of a sense of the Church which has come to Lutheranism has struck Protestantism as a whole. A restudy of Luther, Calvin, and St. Augustine, together with the world crisis, has driven all Protestantism back to the Scriptures. There they have seen again the great fact of the unity of the Church. Some of them have not yet seen that it is a *spiritual* unity which our Lord is calling for, a unity in "one Lord, one faith, one baptism." When the Ecumenical Movement sees that clearly a new day will dawn in the history of the movement. There are many within the movement who see it. But the principle has not yet fully captured the leadership.

---

[3] "Die Reformatorische Lehre von der Kirche," Eberhard Müller, ed. *Wahrheit und Wirklichkeit der Kirche*, p. 122, Berlin: Furche-verlag, 1935.

As we find ourselves in the midst of great financial campaigns to gather millions for the relief of fellow-Christians in war-torn Europe, is it not also the great opportunity for our leaders to drive home to American Protestants this great truth which Luther revived, that the Church is *one,* that it is the fellowship of all believers, that it is the Body of Christ?

The Church continues to look at herself and makes another discovery. She seems to be losing her identity. Instead of being a holy people of God, apart from the world, she has become all too much a part of the world. Is that, too, because she has forgotten what the Church is and what Christ meant it to be? Is it true, as Dr. Pauck has so shockingly said, that the time has come for a secularized church to ask herself, "What must we do to be saved?"[4] It would seem logical that the Church's first step in answering that question should be to rediscover what the Church is. If the progress of the ecumenical movement is a criterion, we may believe that the Protestant churches have begun to face the problem.

Bernhard Iddings Bell has put the issue squarely up to the union movement and asks, "What is the Church? That is the crucial question. . . . Until there is unity about the nature and function of the Church itself, it is impossible that there shall be any real agreement upon minor and derivative matters."[5]

Protestantism, stinging under this flood of indictments, and made conscious finally of what it has lost, has begun to bestir itself. It has begun to scratch beneath the surface of superficial "churchiology" to rediscover

---
[4] Niebuhr, H. R., Miller, F. P., Pauck, Wilhelm, *The Church Against the World*, p. 4. N. Y.: Willett, Clark & Co., 1935.
[5] *A Catholic Looks at His World*, p. 124. N. Y.: Morehouse, 1936.

again the doctrine of the Church and the reality of the Communion of Saints. The Report of the Edinburgh Conference and the documents preparing for Amsterdam show how concerned it is. The very conflict of opinions awakens a dull fear that it may be again, in true Protestant style, every man for himself—every group and every theologian formulating definitions of the Church without regard for what the Church, through the centuries, has already said in the matter on the basis of the Word.

Has the Church no adequate definition of herself? Surely she has, in the New Testament, with the background of the Old. But who is to tell us what the New Testament doctrine of the Church is? Can we let Rome do it? No, because she dares to identify the "Body of Christ" with an organized human machine, which she herself admits has often been seething with corruption. Shall we let Calvin tell us? Hardly, because his idea of the Church as the communion of the predestined is not in harmony with the Scriptural doctrine of the Body of Christ. Can Luther tell us? Yes, because he begins with Scripture and ends with the Creed of the Church, which gives the answer when she confesses, "I believe in the holy Christian Church, the Communion of Saints." It took the Lutheran Reformation to give back to the Church the glorious doctrine of the Communion of Saints, a truth which she had confessed since the time of the apostles, but whose reality and comfort had been lost to the Christians for a thousand years.

Luther revived the doctrine of the Church. But history repeated itself. Came Pietism, came Rationalism, came Schleiermacher, came the sectarian deluge. And when the Church came to herself she rubbed her eyes and asked, "Where is the Church?"

There presents itself an endless array of reasons why this problem must be faced. The relation of Church and State cannot be clarified unless there is first an understanding of what the Church is. It is a question whether the Church will ever again see her obligation of Christian education until she knows herself, and knows what she is. And so could be multiplied the problems of the Church which would in many cases solve themselves, if this basic problem of the Church could be solved.

We turn to Luther to find out what part this idea of the Church played in the Reformation, as well as to learn what the answer of the Reformation was to the problem. There were men before Luther who had seen the need of a reformation. But it was Luther who first saw clearly that at the root of the trouble lay a human and unscriptural conception of the very nature of the Church. When that fact began to dawn on Luther he went to work to define the Church. He left no stone unturned in Scripture and in the Fathers, until up through the years the picture grew clearer and clearer of the Church as one, the Body of Christ, the Communion of Saints. Nothing in all the writings of Luther speaks with more eloquent joy than when he sings the praises of the One Holy Church which has become at length a living reality of boundless comfort in his life. As early as 1520, in the "Tessaradecas Consolatoria," he writes, "This is the communion of saints in which we glory. And whose heart will not be lifted up, even in the midst of great evils, when he believes that which indeed is the very truth; namely, that the blessings of all the saints are his blessings, and that his evil is also theirs!"[6]

---
[6] *The Fourteen of Consolation.* Holman I. 165.

CHAPTER TWO

Luther AND THE ANCIENT TRADITION

BACK TO THE SCRIPTURES

To follow Luther's thinking as he finds his way from the Roman to his own mature definition of the Church, it is necessary to understand his whole approach to doctrinal truth. In the Reformation Luther set out to restore "the Truth of the Gospel" in the Church in order to revive Christian faith and life. Luther's original conception of doctrinal truth was an inheritance. He grew up in the Roman Catholic Church of the 15th century, a child of the Medieval Church, believing as "Mother Church" believed and taught him through priest and teacher. But Luther was not only a Roman Catholic. He was a serious-minded Christian. Under the influence of the Holy Spirit he moved on step by step toward the Christian maturity of a full-grown "man in Christ." It was a painful journey. It led him through years of intellectual and spiritual struggle. The battle was tremendous. It embraced in the first place the daring to question inherited beliefs, and the pain of discovering that they did not all harmonize with divine truth. It further embraced the difficulty of transferring one's court of last appeal from tradition to Holy Writ to determine the truth, and of having to get along without the mediatorship of the Holy Mother and the saints. Getting to heaven without dipping into the convenient treasury of merits of the saints, and having to trust altogether in the merits of Christ could not be endorsed in Rome.

It was like the launching of a huge ocean liner, this spiritual pilgrimage of Luther from Rome to Wittenberg. Sitting comfortably in dry dock in the arms of "Mother Church"; made fast with manifold lines of ecclesiastical rules and rites and easily-performed penances; protected by her power; guaranteed security by her authority—it was altogether a cozy arrangement, not to be given up too lightly.

But when a ship is finished the idea is to get out of dry dock, to cut loose and sail the seas and fight the storms and carry out the purpose for which she was built. When God has created a new man in Christ, He does not expect him to sit in dry dock and rot. He expects him to cut loose and go to sea, to face the storms of life and carry out the purpose for which he was created. God has a right to expect that, because the price of that new creation was the life-blood of His own Son.

Up through his early years Luther enjoyed the security of resting in the faith of the Church. But the high cost of his redemption called to the honest heart of Luther for something more than that. It was *his* life Christ had redeemed. It was *his* faith that bound him to Christ. The faith of the Church must be made his own. But his own faith must be rooted more deeply than in human decrees of popes and councils. Where did they have their roots? The investigation was on. Step by step, doctrine by doctrine, the search for the truth continued.

We do well to remember that this was no cold-blooded

search of an unbeliever carrying on a scientific investigation of different conceptions of truth. It was the search of a child of God. He knew in whom he believed. But he had no peace. His conscience was on fire. The Law stung him with a deep conviction of sin. His righteousness was filthy rags before the awful righteousness of God. How could he pacify such a God with his faltering obedience? The Church said, "Do penance; do this, do that." But his conscience said, "It doesn't help." And like a whipped slave, bleeding under the tyranny of Law, his soul cried out in despair, "Oh, when wilt thou become truly pious and do sufficient to attain to a gracious God?"[1]

He tells later how, as a faithful son of the Church, he continued for years to suffer under this agony of uncertainty, trying vainly to find peace with God under the system of penances, striving to earn his salvation with his good works. "Under the Papacy they inculcated in us that Christ would come as judge, and although they read the Gospel daily, they proclaimed Him as judge and insisted that we should make satisfaction for our sins. To this end they established the saints and Mary as intercessors. Formerly we were thus subject to judgment, and the thought of the Son of God was a cause of terror. If we had known better we should not have gone into the monastery. When I beheld Christ, I seemed to see the devil. Hence the invocation, O Mary, pray for us to thy Son and assuage His anger. Even yet I have trouble daily before I can seize hold of Christ. So strong is the habit of former years. It is an old, evil, rotten tree that has rooted itself in me, for it is a doctrine according to reason that he who commits sin shall make satisfaction for it. This is natural law—if I sin it behooves me to make satisfaction.

---
[1] *Von der heiligen Taufe Predigten D. Mart. Luth.* W. xxxvii, 661.

Thus I lose Christ, the Savior and Consoler, and make of Him the jailer and hangman of my poor soul. Anew we obtain light. But even when I became a doctor I was ignorant of this."[2]

Behind the question, "What is the truth?" lay the other question Luther must solve, "Where shall I find the truth; what is the ultimate source, the final authority?" He sought it in a monastery. He sought it from his brothers in the order. He searched the Fathers. But because he was still a child of God, he was driven on through this maze of human authorities back to the ultimate source of truth, the Word of God. He buried himself in the Scriptures. He studied them, he translated them, he preached them, he paraphrased them in hymns, he taught them, he summarized them in the Catechism. Like an octopus they took hold of him, inch by inch overpowering him, until finally all his thinking and preaching revolved within the orbit of revealed truth. From then on he was an instrument of God, and the Reformation became God's work. It was such a man who stood at the Diet of Worms before the Emperor and all the power of Rome, refusing to recant a word of his writings; for as he said, "I am held fast by the Scriptures adduced by me, and my conscience is taken captive by God's Word, and I neither can nor will revoke anything, seeing that it is neither safe nor right to act against conscience. God help me. Amen."[3]

When this conviction, long before Worms, dawned on Luther, that the Scriptures were the final and absolute authority, we might have expected that Luther would at

---
[2]*Predigt am Pfingstmontag*, W. XLV, 86, 1537.
[3]*Verhandlungen mit D. Martin Luther auf dem Reichstage zu Worms.* W. vii, 877, 1521.

once step out of the organized church, anathemize tradition, and start a new "church." That was virtually what some of the "Protestant Reformers" did. But that was not Luther's way. Luther had a keen understanding of history, a fine regard for tradition, a deep reverence for his teachers and the Fathers, and a burning love for the Church of Christ. But this "Church," what was it? Was it this hierarchical organization, with a corrupt head at Rome calling himself the vicar of Christ, claiming all power in temporal things as well as spiritual? If it was, then it was not his to question, but his to obey with a blind obedience. But was that the "Church"?

Luther could not go far in his search of the Scriptures before that question began to trouble him. And he soon realized that his solution of that question would determine his whole relation to the Roman Catholic Church. He set about examining the problem. And that investigation is the story of the evolution of Luther's concept of the Church. It is that story which seeks to be told in these pages.

TRADITION VERSUS *THE TRADITION*

Luther had arrived at the ultimate source of truth. But what of this other authority which his church had placed side by side with the Scriptures? What of tradition? Would he dare to cast that aside? Was it of no value? Did it have no authority whatever? And what was it, this thing called tradition? In clarifying the doctrine of the Church, could he disregard teachers, Church Fathers, history, age-old practice, tradition? Certainly not. But traditions are one thing, and *the tradition* is another. Luther's keen historical insight told him, as a teacher sent from God, that there is a tradition—call it the teaching tradition (without Roman implications),[4] or anything you like—which has its roots in Scripture. Its basic content is what Moffatt calls the "sacred deposit,"[5] or what Jude in his Epistle calls "the faith which was once delivered unto the saints." That "faith," or "sacred deposit" is the objective teaching of Scripture. It is summarized and defined by the Church in its teaching. This "body of Scriptural doctrine" is the genuine doctrinal tradition. In the Apostolic Church we see it in its original, elemental and pure form. This tradition continues to live in the Church like the trunk of a great tree. Up through the centuries branches grow on the trunk. Many of them are legitimate, healthy branches: implications and applications of the Scriptural doctrine. The Holy Spirit is active in the Church, creating and sustaining life, giving growth, causing fruits of faith to spring.

Up through the same centuries, however, there begin to appear parasites, suckers, unhealthy growths, which prey upon the tree and suck the vital sap out of it, impairing both its health and its beauty. These parasites in the life of the Church are the human traditions. They are creations of men, additions to the original tradition. They may be harmless, even helpful, when they touch secondary matters like forms of worship and the like. But when they pile up and begin to disturb the doctrines of the faith they become a serious threat. They may mar the beauty and undermine the health of the Church, for as Luther said, some of them are neither borne out by Scripture nor are they in accord with Scripture. When that has taken place in any church group, one can no longer talk about "the tradition." One must talk about

---

[4] Cf. Karl Adam, *Spirit of Catholicism*. London: Sheed & Ward, 1937.
[5] James Moffatt, *The Thrill of Tradition*, p. 109. N. Y.: Macmillan, 1944.

"traditions." For the genuine tradition has been hidden; it has been enlarged, altered, violated. Then there is only one thing that will restore the tradition. Reformation! And Reformation means repentance and renewal. It means clearing away the accumulated rubbish of human traditions and going back to let God speak to His Church again through His holy Word. That was the operation Luther was called on to perform in the Church. That was the Reformation.

Martin Luther was born into a church whose leaders prattled proudly about the tradition which they and they alone possessed. But when they spoke of the tradition they meant the accumulated body of human traditions which had grown up like an undisciplined grapevine through fifteen centuries. Luther's keen eye saw that his task was to trim down that inflated tradition until there was nothing left but the simple old apostolic tradition itself. Not that he recklessly cast aside every tradition which was not specifically commanded in Scripture. He left that method to the Enthusiasts. Luther clung tenaciously to the ancient practices of the Mother Church. The "funded experience"[6] of the Church was sacred with Luther, and he only dared examine it with the greatest reverence. But examine it he must to see that it was in all points in harmony with Scripture.

That checking process was a process of a lifetime for Luther, as it must be for every serious-minded Christian. For, as the eminent Luther scholar, Wilhelm Walther, says, "Our religious possession has two elements: first, what we have acknowledged as individuals through our own experience of the truth, and second, what we recognize as truth as members of Christendom (Christenheit)

---

[6] A significant term used by Moffatt, *op. cit.*, p. 110.

on the basis of the experience of other believers."[7] Luther never questioned that the individual must himself come to conviction as to what is the truth, as he stands face to face with God in His Word. A man can do that without searching history to see what the Church has always believed. But he is gambling. And gambling is a hazardous business, especially when the stakes are a man's eternal destiny. A man may be too naive or too proud to ask what the Church believes, and go it alone in his search for truth. But there is always the chance that he may come to the wrong conviction. It might help if he "checked" with the Church. History is full of the pathetic examples of those who have insisted on finding God's truth in the Bible without reference to what the Church has believed through the ages. And we see the results in the religious casualties all along the road of the past: sects, fanatics, heretics, who have come upon the religious scene and gone, to leave behind them only a flurry of confusion, disillusionment and tragedy.

And it must be so. For the individualist is guided only by his own meager experience. The Church is guided by the experience of millions, including the experience of many great saints and teachers. He bases his conclusions on his own religious knowledge and insight. The Church bases hers on the insight of the whole people of God through the centuries. "Of course, what I have experienced myself will appear to me as a much surer basis for my conviction than what others have experienced. But it is not thereby proven that the former is more sure and dependable than the latter. Certainly, what the Christian really experiences because of his harmony with the objective Word of God and the testimony of the Holy Spirit

---

[7]*Das Erbe der Reformation*, Vol. I, p. 24. Leipzig: Deichert, 1917.

can become absolute certainty. But who does not recognize the possibility of misunderstandings of Scripture and a confusion of one's own spirit with the Holy Spirit? In short, if I had the choice of trusting either the experience of all believers of the past or of my own experience, I would choose the former."[8] But, says Walther, it is not a matter of either-or. Luther struck the right balance between man as an individual before God, and man as a member of the whole Body. He is first a member of the Body. He inherits the whole spiritual treasure of the Church to begin with in holy Baptism and through the accompanying Word up through the years. But as he grows in insight and experience and makes this inheritance his own, he becomes able to prove the faith he has received and, if necessary, eliminate the errors he may discover. This is the work of a lifetime. For he is dealing with the experience of a multitude of saints, who have fought battles and grappled with problems of which he may long remain ignorant.

And so the balanced Christian recognizes both of these sources of his religious faith and life. He is a fool if he disregards his inheritance and the judgment of the Church. He is lost if he receives it and does not make it his own. In the latter case he is a hypocrite. In the former he is what church history calls a sectarian, and what St. Paul calls a schismatic. Luther was neither. His worst enemies will not call him a hypocrite. That would be preferable; for that is too absurd to take seriously or to do any harm. But there are unhappily those who call him a sectarian. That is more damaging, because it is more plausible to anyone who knows just a smattering of history. It looks at first blush almost as if Luther broke the

---
[8] *Ibid.*, p. 23

unity of the Church and started the whole movement which broke up into the multitude of sects and denominations and groups which constitute the present ecclesiastical chaos. But a little sanity of thinking will tell us that it is one thing to set free a camp of American prisoners in Japan; and another thing to turn them into a vengeful mob, killing, pillaging and burning the whole city. The one is right and noble. The other is murder.

No one can understand Luther's position in this development unless he understands the one basic fact, that the Church is *one*. With that fundamental fact in mind Luther carried out the Reformation, not as a schismatic movement, but as a cleansing movement within the Church. It was those who went beyond him who carried it away into schism and sectarianism. Luther proclaimed again the principle of Christian freedom. But the Enthusiasts turned it into license. Luther knew only *one* Church. The others were interested only in "churches."

Luther represented everything that is contrary to sectarianism. He was a man of the Church. He was a faithful member of the organized Church. He opposed every effort to split the Church. He did not wish to break away from the Church. The last thing he wanted was to form a new "church," which to him represented schism and therefore sin. What he did want was to bring about a cleansing of the Church "in head and members," and to do it through the proper channels of reform. He appealed first to the Bishops; then to the Pope; then to a General Council. That was the normal way to bring about reform.

When the great threat of schism came to the Early Church, the Council of Nicea was called. It was a representative assembly of the greatest spirits in the Church. Both sides were heard. But under the prayerful leadership of inspired Christian men the truth prevailed. Schism on a grand scale was averted and the unity of the Church preserved. And we are all satisfied that the Holy Spirit was present and guided the deliberations to a right outcome.

But when the great threat to unity came with Luther, no General Council was called to gather all the great spiritual leaders of the Church. No opportunity was given for Luther the "heretic" to present his case, nor for the Church to be fairly apprised of the issue. A political Diet was called, a "packed" assembly, if there ever was one. Emperor and Pope marshalling their might and telling Luther, "Recant, or else!" No effort was made to judge the case fairly on the basis of the Scriptures. Only, "Recant or burn!"

When Luther refused to retract, because he stood on the firm ground of Scripture, which his opponents refused to hear, they made the grand gesture: they excommunicated him! Luther, and soon millions with him, were solemnly read out of the fellowship of the organized Church. But when Luther burned the Bull of Excommunication, he was saying in unmistakable terms to Rome and to the world that he was neither a heretic nor a schismatic. He was not a sectarian. He was a man of the Church. He was saying what he said to Rome in so many words years later, "We are the true ancient Church, and with the entire holy Christian Church we are one Body and a Communion of Saints. . . . You are the new, false church, apostate from the ancient true Church."[9] In other words, he is saying to Rome, "We have not broken the unity of the Church, you have."

But someone will say, "Isn't that just big talk?" The

[9] *Wider Hans Worst,* W. LI, 487, 1541.

answer is, that it makes sense only when we realize that Luther had arrived at a deeper conception of *what the Church is* than his Roman persecutors. Their idea of the Church had degenerated into an organization complex. St. Paul's "Body of Christ" and the Early Church's "Communion of Saints" had shriveled through those dark centuries into an organization, a hierarchy, whose membership was determined by a signing on the dotted line.

Luther, brought face to face with the threat of excommunication, was compelled, both for his own peace of mind and for the welfare of the Church, to think through the whole conception of the nature of the Church. "What is the Church?" Through this investigation he discovers again where his roots are. They are buried deep in the same ground wherein he found the doctrine of justification by faith and all the other doctrines that were crying out for life: deep in the New Testament. He found them in St. Paul's *soma Christou* and *koinonia*, the Body of Christ and the communion, or fellowship. He found them in the "Communio Sanctorum" of the Early Church. He found them in the Church Fathers—above all, in St. Augustine.

As Luther traced that truth of St. Paul up through the centuries he got hold of the red thread, the original tradition, the Scriptural doctrine of the Church; and he followed it all the way up. He saw it run through the Early Church; through Nicea; through the early controversies; through St. Augustine; through the Apostles' and the Athanasian creeds. Then down it went into a valley of confusion, growing darker through the centuries. Each century seemed to pile up new errors, conspiring to conceal the truth.

But down there in the valley Luther found men who

had gone before him, faithful men digging like deep-sea divers trying to uncover a lost cable, each of them clearing away a little debris, bringing a little more of the truth to light. These were the men who kept alive *the tradition*. And that tradition Luther laid hold on, and lending his inspired power to the task he brought the cable of truth into the light of day again in that world-shaking event and miracle of God which was the Reformation.

THE TRADITION FROM ST. PAUL TO LUTHER

Our task is not to try to determine the New Testament doctrine of the Church through an original study of the Scriptures. Our task is to get at Luther's conception of that doctrine. To do that it is necessary only to present the simple elements of the doctrine as it is taught in the New Testament, elements on which the whole Church is pretty well agreed. That elemental doctrine was held and practiced by the Apostolic Church. But as time moves on the *koinonia,* or fellowship, of those early Christians becomes more and more organized, systematized, formalized. An intricate church polity grows up. The simple faith of the early Christian community is disturbed by heretics and false teachers. It becomes necessary to defend the faith. And that means to define it. And so there grows up necessarily a system of dogma. The "faith once for all delivered to the saints" is defined in details sufficient to meet the attacks of every new heresy. We can hardly conceive of it being otherwise.

In that process the doctrine of the Church, too, is defined in more and more detail. For there is growing up an ecclesiastical juggernaut, an outward organization, a hierarchy, which claims to be the Church of God, and whose human head residing in Rome calls himself the vicar of Christ with supreme power over both the Church and the State. It took centuries for the simple spiritual New Testament conception of the Church in the first century to grow into that intricate, worldly, hierarchical conception which faced Luther when he appeared on the scene of history. The original tradition was embellished, changed, and profaned, and human traditions took the place of the inspired and revealed tradition of the Apostolic Church.

The picture of the Church which Luther finds in the New Testament is painted with particular beauty and fullness by St. Paul. It is clear from his and the other New Testament writings that there is *one* Church which is *God's own creation*. Whether in the Old Testament or the New the Church is *God's people (laos Theou)*.[10] God Himself chose Israel to be His people. He entered into covenant with them and sealed the covenant with the blood of His own Son, typified in the bloody sacrifices of the Old Testament. By faith in the promised Messiah (Heb. 11) they could become members of the true spiritual Israel. That is the "Israel according to the spirit" which St. Paul by implication contrasts with the "Israel according to the flesh" (I Cor. 10:18) and identifies with the Church. "For they are not all Israel, which are of Israel" (Rom. 9:6). But there is a "remnant" of the faithful (Micah 2:12; Jer. 23:3), a conception of the Church of God which carries over from the Old Testament to the New. For Isaiah says, "Though thy people Israel be as the sand of the sea, yet a remnant of them shall return" (10:22). And St. Paul, picking up Isaiah's prophecy echoes, "A remnant shall be saved" (Rom. 9:22). For, says the Apostle, "even so at this present time also there

---

[10] Exodus 3:7, 10; Acts 7:34ff.; I Peter 2:10.

is a remnant according to the election of grace" (Rom. 11:5). The Church of God is *one*. It is God's people of all times. There is an unbroken *continuity* between the Church of the Old Testament and that of the New, "since the God of the Old Covenant, who then established the New Covenant, speaks in Christ, and the New Testament assembly (Versammlung) of God in Christ is nothing else than the fulfilled Old Testament assembly of God."[11]

A perfect picture of that unity and continuity of the Church in the Old and the New is given us in St. Stephen's apology in Acts 7. The martyr quotes Exodus 3:5ff., where the Lord says to Moses, "I have seen the affliction of my people . . . I will send thee into Egypt." Then St. Stephen goes on to say, "This is he, that was in the church in the wilderness" (Acts 7:34-38). "God's People" of the Old Testament, says St. Stephen, was the Church.

Thus the *oneness* of the Church is everywhere apparent from Scripture. At the first stages of the New Testament Church's development there arose the painful dispute as to whether the Gentiles could be members of the Church equally with the Jews. St. Paul smashed that sectarian conception of the Church and cried out in a hundred different ways, that the Church is *one!* "For ye are all the children of God by faith in Christ Jesus. For as many of you as have been baptized into Christ have put on Christ. There is neither Jew nor Greek, there is neither bond nor free, there is neither male nor female: for ye are all *one* in Christ Jesus. And if ye be Christ's, then are ye Abraham's seed, and heirs according to the promise" (Gal. 3:26-29). That declaration, together with

---

[11]K. L. Schmidt cited by Gerhard Kittel in *Theologisches Wörterbuch zum Neuen Testament*, Vol. III, p. 515. Stuttgart: Kohlhammer, 1938.

scores of others in the New Testament, made Christ the heart and center of the Church. And membership in it was not a matter of being a son of Abraham "according to the flesh," but of the spiritual seed of Abraham. And whether Jew or Gentile that membership in the Church was determined by faith in Christ, the Messiah.

That faith bound the believers together in such unity and in such an intimate fellowship with Christ that St. Paul calls them the "Body of Christ" (Eph. 1:22). And since we are members of His Body by faith, we are at the same time made "members one of another" (Rom. 5:12). This is no mere physical-sociological proposition. It is in essence a spiritual phenomenon. For the faith through which Christ holds them together is spiritual, and only God can surely know where true faith exists.

There is here, then, what the Early Church called a *koinonia,* a *fellowship of believers,* or a *communion of saints.* The fellowship was primarily and basically a communion with Christ through faith. Out of that relationship grew the fellowship of believers with one another through a common faith. And the Church could confess with St. Paul, "There is one body, and one Spirit, even as ye are called in one hope of your calling; one Lord, one faith, one baptism, one God and Father of all, who is above all, and through all, and in you all" (Eph. 4:4-6).

Hence there is a fellowship of faith (Eph. 4:13), of worship and sacramental life and prayer (Acts 2:42); a fellowship of love, of sharing and suffering (Rom. 12:15; I Cor. 11:29; Gal. 6:2). All this expresses itself indeed in an outward corporate life and community. But the essence of it is spiritual. A communistic society at its best is not the Church. The Church is the Body of Christ to which belong not those who give what they have to others but those who believe in Jesus Christ. If they believe in Christ and therefore are in the Church, they will live in a fellowship of love, they will share with others and bear the burdens one of another. But there must first be the Church, the inner spiritual communion of souls who by faith in Christ are made members one of another in the Body of Christ. That is St. Peter's "spiritual house" (I Peter 2:5), the "chosen generation, a royal priesthood, an holy nation, a peculiar people; . . . which in time past were not a people, but are now the people of God" (2: 9-10). That is St. Paul's "household of God" where we are "fellow citizens with the saints"; God's temple, "built upon the foundation of the apostles and prophets, Jesus Christ Himself being the chief cornerstone; in whom all the building fitly framed together groweth unto an holy temple in the Lord: in whom ye also are builded together for an habitation of God through the Spirit" (Eph. 2: 19-22).

That is the Church, the *ekklesia* of God. And when this Body of Christ, this spiritual fellowship of believers, manifests its presence in local congregations and outward communities, it does not change the fact that in essence the Church is still the *spiritual* Communion of Saints in which we believe. The failure to keep that fact clear is the basic reason behind the birth and development of the hierarchical conception of Rome. And it was on that line that the battle of the Reformation must be fought. Luther found that he must emancipate the Church of God from its hierarchical fetters, and restore again the sense of the Communion of Saints in the Body of Christ. No Christian must henceforth live in the fear of damnation because he refuses to recognize a corrupt Roman bishop as the vicar of Christ and the keeper of his soul. No believer in Christ must be robbed of his freedom in the Gospel to become a slave to the new Judaism of Rome.

It is easy to see that at the heart of that struggle must lie the basic doctrine of justification by faith. When that doctrine was clarified, it became self-evident to Luther that since his relation to God was one of grace, there was no place for a conception of the Church which made membership in it depend on a legalistic obedience to outward rules and regulations. For the Church is the fellowship of all believers, the communion of all those who have been justified by grace through faith in Jesus Christ.

The simple New Testament conception of the Communion of Saints which the Early Church enjoyed had in it one element which was soon to be shamefully abused. There was a communion of saints, not only *with* one another, but *for* one another. The believers were to serve one another, bear one another's burdens, pray for one another, die for one another. And it was especially this idea of intercession that was magnified, and the idea that through our holiness we can store up treasure for the benefit of others. The new element which had crept in and taken root before it could be stopped, was the idea of *merit*, human merit, as opposed to the all-sufficiency of the merits of Christ.

The foundations for the tower of Babel are laid early, being apparent already in the second century. The tower rises: intercessions of the saints and the Virgin, the sacrifice of the Mass, indulgences, purgatory, treasury of merits, supererrogation.

And so the story goes on into the Middle Ages and up to the day of Luther.

Luther was by no means the first one to devote himself to this difficult problem. The line of great predecessors in this field goes way back to the Early Fathers. Cyprian and Augustine wrestled with the problem, but were already enmeshed in the net which was to cradle the Roman conception of the Church as a visible hierarchical institution.

Cyprian said, "There is one God, and Christ is one, and there is one Church, and one chair founded upon the rock by the word of the Lord."[12]

Augustine's study of the question has been basic for all later discussion of the subject. There is an unhappy conflict in his statements which makes it difficult to follow him to his conclusion. He speaks at times of an *invisibilis caritatis compages,* a structure or communion of invisible grace. The Church is a communion of true believers alone. But this spiritual Church is only to be found within the visible Catholic Church. And outside of this visible Church there is no Church. When Augustine said, "I would indeed not believe the Gospel, unless the authority of the catholic Church moved me," he never knew that he would be used as a pillar for that ecclesiastical structure, which has become the hierarchy of Rome.

The enemy sowed tares in that innocent seed of Cyprian and Augustine. Without knowing it, they had sown the wind. The Church reaped the whirlwind. Sweeping down through the centuries, it touches off the blare of Roman trumpets, as Innocence the Third exalts the Papacy to dizzy pinnacles of power. The holy Mother Church alone stands firm, and only confusion results from a diversity of religions. Falsehood and truth, peril-

---

[12]"To the People, Concerning Five Schismatic Presbyters of the Faction of Felicissimus." *Ante-Nicene Fathers,* Vol. V, p. 318. N. Y.: Scribner, 1896-99.

ously mixed together, until the hierarchical conception has all but driven the idea of the Communion of Saints from the field.

No, not altogether. For even the Roman theologians have made use of the formula—how can they help it, since it refuses to disappear from the Creed? But always, like Augustine, they proceed to shut up the Communion of Saints within the Roman Catholic Church, with certain well-defined exceptions.

The *Scholastics* picked it up where Augustine laid it down. Hugo of St. Victor called the Church the *"multitudo fidelium universitas Christianorum,"* the multitude of the faithful, the world of Christians. To Thomas Aquinas it was the *"communio fidelium,"* the communion of the faithful. But always these were to be found only within the Catholic Church. Therefore the Catholic Church is the true Church of Christ, through which the Spirit works and by which salvation is dispensed. This body is infallible and at its head is the Pope, in whom is a plenitude of power in the Church. Since the hope of salvation depends on outward membership in the institution, the question for every individual is, not primarily obedience to Christ, but obedience to the Roman Church. For the Church is the dispenser of damnation as well as salvation.

The most extravagant claims of power ever made by Rome came with the Bull *"Unam Sanctam"* of Boniface VIII. There is only one holy, catholic church. Absolute submission in faith to this church is necessary, for outside of it there is neither salvation, nor remission of sin.

This pretentious manifesto appeared two hundred years before Luther. Yet the year before Luther posted his 95 Theses Pope Leo X declared the Bull to be in full force and effect. This document answers the question which poses itself at this point, *"Where was the Church when Luther arrived?"*

With the perspective of centuries, Luther seemed to see what we can see now, looking back at the Church of Luther's day. The free communion of the followers of Jesus had grown into an enormous temporal organization. Individual communion with God had given place to blind obedience to the Church, which to the layman meant obedience to the priest, the bishop, the Pope at Rome. Personal devotion to Christ had yielded to a mechanical religion of works and ceremonies. Liberty of conscience had abdicated in favor of an ecclesiastical pawnshop of souls. Is it surprising that Luther at long last saw the need of a campaign of Reformation on this front, too, that he might rescue the New Testament conception of the Church from the hierarchical debris which was smothering it?

We must not suppose that this hierarchical development was never questioned until Luther came. The international sway of the Papacy had been checked by the awakening of a national consciousness, in the German people most of all. The sharp criticism of the Nominalists had taken its toll. Both Marsilius and Occam had challenged the authority of the Church and the Papacy. The latter, they said, was a purely human institution. As in the State, so in the Church, the sovereignty is in the people. The Church of the New Testament is the communion of the faithful, which is built upon Christ and not upon Peter. By establishing Scripture as the highest and only infallible authority in the Church, Nominalism put a wedge in the side of the curial system, which Luther only had to drive in further.

The great Reform Councils, inspired by Gerson, D'Ailly, and others, had given the Papacy a temporary check by proclaiming the supremacy of a general council.

Humanism, for better or for worse, had liberated many consciences from ecclesiastical tyranny. By encouraging free research and the return to original sources, a basis was laid for historical criticism. The effect of this on the traditional authority of the Church is self-evident. Decretals and fabrications, long since composed in support of hierarchical authority crumbled while the Papacy groaned. But because Humanism was an intellectual, rather than a spiritual, renaissance, it failed where Luther succeeded.

A more positive preparation for Luther's doctrine of the Church was made by later forerunners of the Reformation. Wesel and Wessel continued where Marsilius and Occam had begun. The nature of the Church, they said, is spiritual, and its unity consists in a community of its members in one faith, forming a Communion of Saints with one Head, Jesus Christ.

Wyclif and Hus went deeper than all the others in defining the nature of the Church. But their very definition of the Church as the *congregatio ómnium praedestinatorum,* congregation of all the elect, was unfortunate, since it included the elect of all time, past, present and future. The Church would then be a congregation not only of Christians but also of blaspheming Sauls who, while not yet converted, nevertheless were of the elect. Since it was inconceivable that the latter could belong to the Communion of Saints, the doctrine of the Church in Wyclif and Hus was inadequate to replace the hierarchical conception. They could shake, but not shatter, the Roman doctrine of the Church.

In a recently discovered manuscript of the late Dr. Albert Hauck, the great historian of Leipzig makes this statement regarding the forerunners of Luther:

"None of these tendencies nor these men really knew the answer to the question: What is the Church? For the answer was conditioned by a new conception of faith. . . . This became the Reformation, and thus the Reformation brought us the true evangelical conception of the Church."[13]

---

[13] "Gegensätze im Kirchenbegriff des späteren Mittelalters," *Luthertum*, 1938, Heft 8, p. 240.

Part Two

LUTHER THE ROMAN CATHOLIC

CHAPTER THREE

Luther THE OBEDIENT SON

HIS EARLY ENVIRONMENT AND THE DOCTRINE OF THE CHURCH

The preceding glimpse of the Church's history has revealed two distinct tendencies in the development of the doctrine of the Church. The one identifies it with the Roman hierarchy, the other conceives it as a spiritual communion. The question naturally arises: In which milieu did Luther grow to spiritual and theological maturity? It is easy to say that his doctrine of the Church was merely a product of his environment and a rehashing of the ideas of his predecessors. Grisar makes that superficial estimate of Luther's thinking, when he heads a paragraph in his *Luther*, "The little world of Wittenberg and the great world in Church and State."[1] Here he intimates that Luther was so steeped in the liberal humanistic environment of Wittenberg that his defection was a natural result of this local contamination. But Grisar himself admits that the religious atmosphere at Wittenberg was wholly Catholic.[2] The briefest glance at Luther's early

---
[1]*Luther* . . . authorized tr. from the German by E. M. Lamond, Vol. I, p. 37. London: K. Paul, Trench, Trübner & Co., Ltd., 1913-17.
[2]*Ibid.*, p. 30.

years suffices to show that he grew up in the strict atmosphere of traditional Catholicism.

Luther's boyhood and youth were years of uncompromising discipline. His home and the schools of Mansfeld, Magdeburg, and Eisenach used the rod mercilessly. The climax was reached in the monastery at Erfurt, where the vow of obedience stood side by side with the vows of poverty and chastity.

His training in obedience, though received according to the Commandment, nevertheless left its deep mark on Luther. As the rod of the teacher held him in constant fear of corporal punishment, so the rod of divine law which was so harshly administered in home and cloister threatened him with his soul's perdition. Through perfect obedience to parent and teacher he could avoid the rod. Likewise, through perfect obedience to the precepts of God and the Holy Church he could avoid eternal punishment.

Thus we find Luther growing up in an atmosphere of physical and spiritual tyranny. Not that that was unusual. He was not alone, either in suffering under it or in his inclination to question its propriety. Erasmus and other Humanists had already thrown off the shackles which had so long bound the minds of men. But theirs was not the answer in the religious realm, even if it might appear to be in the intellectual. The application of the Humanist remedy in the Church is perhaps more to blame than anything else in history for the individual "liberty à la license," which is eating the very heart out of Protestantism today. A stronger force than Humanism was necessary for the emancipation of the souls of the sixteenth century from ecclesiastical and Judaistic tyranny.

We must not think that Luther in his early years was conscious of this tyranny, any more than the great mass of his fellow Christians. For centuries men had unconsciously surrendered their spiritual, if not their intellectual, life and growth to the guidance of Mother Church. And let no one cease to pray for the return of that day. But with it there must be a Church that is worthy to be called "Mother." Luther was a true son of that regime. He clung to Mother Church long after he began to attack abuses within the Church. It was long before he would allow himself to believe that his dear Mother Church had been ravished by a corrupt clergy. The day came when he saw the light and knew that the true Mother Church was the Communion of Saints. Then he needed no longer hesitate to throw all his God-given powers into the fight to emancipate his holy Mother from her worldly captors. But not yet. His early works testify unquestionably to the fact that Luther grew to maturity as a good Catholic, reared in the traditional life and doctrine of the Catholic Church.

FIRST STAGES IN LUTHER'S DOCTRINE OF THE CHURCH

The first stage in the development of Luther's doctrine of the Church takes us to the beginning of the Indulgence Controversy. It brings us through those significant years from 1513 to 1516, when Luther was lecturing on the Psalms and Romans. His spiritual rebirth, which he later speaks of, had taken place. Whether it took place in the monastery at Erfurt or during the year preceding the lectures on the Psalms of 1513-1516 does not concern us here. Certain it is that the doctrine of the Church in Luther does not mature until the basic idea of justification by faith has taken complete possession of him. The latter marked Luther's spiritual emancipation. It was the light which clarified every other Bible doctrine to him.

In the blessed Word of justification by faith Luther had found the point of contact between the soul and God. But it was more than a matter for the individual soul. Luther did not stop there, but went on to draw all the consequences of this doctrine. The communion of the individual soul with God translates itself into a communion with other souls of like faith. These souls have need of mutual comfort and encouragement. Still more, they have need of the nourishment of the Word of Grace. No more than the early Christians could walk in solitary communion with God could Luther and other justified souls avoid the consciousness that they were part of a community. This community was the Church.

Luther's doctrinal development was a gradual process. That makes it impossible to say that his doctrine of the Church appeared defined at any given moment in his life. He was so steeped in the traditional doctrine that one cannot say with respect to this doctrine that one day he was a "Roman" and the next a "Lutheran."

It is in the "Lectures on the Psalms" that the conflict of the two conceptions of the Church first clearly appears. An expression is thrown out from time to time before that, but the first serious study of the doctrine appears in the "Psalms." And so for our purpose the "Lectures on the Psalms" is the all-important work of this first period. Scholars like Holl, Jundt, and Seeberg agree that these lectures contain everything new that Luther had to say on the doctrine of the Church up to 1517.[3]

These lectures show us on the one hand Luther, the obedient son of Rome, virtually identifying the Church of Christ with the Roman Catholic Church. On the other hand come the first ringing strains of the old refrain, which makes the Church a spiritual communion of all believers in Christ. The refrain, indeed, had never been fully understood, fenced in as it was within the limits of the hierarchical institution. The task for Luther was to define the relation between these two concepts. Were there two churches? Was one a part of the other? Was one only an outward manifestation of the other? The "Lectures on the Psalms" show Luther coming to grips with this basic problem, which no Reformer could possibly sidestep.

[3] Karl Holl, *Gesammelte Aufsätze zur Kirchengeschichte*, Vol. I, p. 306. Tübingen: J. C. B. Mohr, 1927.
Andre Jundt, *Le Developpement de la Pensée Religieuse de Luther jusqu'en 1517*, p. 217. Paris: Libraire Fischbacher, 1906.
Reinhold Seeberg, *Lehrbuch der Dogmengeschichte*, Vol. IV, p. 278. Leipzig: A. Deichert, 1908-23.

CHAPTER FOUR

Luther THE CATHOLIC CRITIC

LECTURES ON THE PSALMS

Too little research has been spent on the "Lectures on the Psalms." When we study that early work of Luther, before 1517, we cannot help wondering at two or three things. The first is that in almost every Lecture we can hear distant echoes of the "voice in the wilderness," the voice of the Reformer that soon was to shake the foundations of the hierarchy. The second surprising thing is, that Luther could talk so much like a Reformer and still be apparently unconscious that he was out of step with his Church body. In the third place the Lectures make us wonder how Rome could fail to see the spark of "heresy," and stamp it out before it became the conflagration which was the Reformation.

One of the first things that revealed Luther's changing attitude toward the Roman conception of the Church was his changing language concerning authority in the Church. In the "Psalms" he is still a good Catholic. He has no quarrel with the Church about the doctrine of the Church. He doesn't question the authority of Pope or Council or prelate or of the Church itself. So far from attacking this authority, he defends it against heretics and schismatics. Don't they know that *"the church cannot err,* while any man can err in his own devotion." ... "It is permitted to no one to follow his own judgment. ... But the authority of the Church, and the understanding ought to be taken captive in obedience to Christ."¹

Quite different, this Luther, urging men to submit implicitly to the Church's interpretation of Scripture, from the Luther who opposed Eck at Leipzig a few years later! Now he makes the bold statement that the Church cannot err. So it is not for the individual to judge whether a doctrine is true or false. It was true that errors had crept in, yes, had "deluged" the Church.² But these are not the errors of the Church, but rather errors against the Church by proud members not content with the traditional doctrines. The heretics, he says on Ps. 100, reject the proof of centuries, the blood of martyrs, and the testimony of Scriptures,³ all of which testify that *the Roman Catholic Church is the one true Church of Christ.* That sounds as much like Eck as Luther. Here the Reformer denies the heretics the right which he later claimed at Leipzig, the right of direct approach to God and of individual interpretation of Scripture with Scripture. The Church which he later saw as a stumbling-block to personal communion with God, he now sees as the "tabernacle" where the faithful might find shelter "from the strife of tongues," *i.e.,* from the attacks of heretics.⁴ Luther's submission to the authority of the Mother Church is complete.

The same obedience is due to the authority of the

---
¹*Decem Praecepta Wittenbergensi praedicato populo.* W. I, 444, L. 14.
²*Ibid,* 418, L. 18
³Ps. 100 (101), W. IV, 129, L. 10.
⁴Ps. 30, 21. W. III, 171, L. 15.

prelates of the Church, who are the vicars of Christ, the altars of the Church, bringing their people as a sacrifice to the Lord.[5] They are not to be despised, but obeyed;[6] for they are by Christ ordained to be rulers over the Church.[7] They are at once the rulers and protectors of the faithful. "Why are priests honored?" he asks in his sermon, "De sacerdotum dignitate Sermo."[8] "I answer: Because their tongues are the keys of the kingdom of the heavens." "Therefore let a man diligently beware, lest he ever discuss or pass judgment on a decision of his prelate."[9]

There is only one step from such submission to Church and prelates to submission to the *Pope*. This is not the place to discuss at length Luther's relation to the Papacy. But it does throw light on his deepening conception of the Church. His obedience to the Papacy is as unquestioned as it is to the Church. He is a good Catholic and a good Papist. In a sermon of 1516 he says, "All the works and merits of Christ and the Church are in the hand of the Pope."[10, 11] "Had Christ not given all His power to man," he says in his "Sermo in vincula Sancti Petri," "there would have been no complete Church, for there would have been no order, since anyone who wished could say that he was moved by the Holy Ghost."[12]

We must conclude from all this that Luther's submission to the authority of the Church, and of Pope and prelates, is complete at this stage. The hierarchy does not

---
[5] Ps. 83, 4. W. III, 646, 645.
[6] Ps. 43. W. III, 248.
[7] Ps. 67, 15. W. III, 386.
[8] W. LV, 657, L. 31.
[9] Ps. 1. W. III, 18, L. 33.
[10] Ps. 102, 20. W. IV, 165.
[11] *Ex Sermone habite Domin. X. post Trinit.* A. 1516, W. I, 67.
[12] W. I, 69.

offend. On the contrary, the very existence and growth of the Church he considers bound up with the hierarchy, with its seat at Rome.[13] The Roman Church holds this position by virtue of the fact that it has remained faithful.[14]

There is one sentence in the Lecture on Ps. 86, quoted above, which catches our attention. It tells us that Luther did not at this time identify the Communion of Saints with the Roman Church, nor exclude the possibility of other church bodies being within the spiritual Church of God. It is the phrase, "Ecclesia Romana, capitalis pars Ecclesiarum omnium," "the Roman Church, the principal part of all churches." We shall recall this a little later, when we discuss the nature of the Church as conceived in these "Lectures on the Psalms."

While Luther thus recognizes the authority of the Church and its offices, he begins even now to unleash his power against the corruption of the spiritual leaders in office and elsewhere. In every estate of the Church, be it laity, clergy, or papacy, corruption has crept in and made the Church sick. The sufferings of the Lord depicted in Ps. 68 (69) reflect the sufferings of His Church.[15] There is indifference, hypocrisy, and spiritual laziness, and the way to heaven is made easy through indulgences and lax teaching. And the blame for the ugly situation lies mainly with the clergy and the leaders in the Church, whose avarice is beyond the imagination of men.

The sin of the clergy is in life and in preaching. Their life is smeared with avarice, even in their pastoral activities. Long before the "95 Theses" Luther had begun to

---
[13]Ps. 86 (87), 4. W. IV, 25.
[14]Ps. 90, 1. W. IV, 65. L. 20.
[15]W. III, 416. 1. 17.

thunder against the revolting sale of indulgences. In the "Sermon on the Tenth Sunday after Trinity" (1516) he does not summarily condemn indulgences. They are indeed the merits of Christ and the saints, and as such ought to be respected and honored. But they have become an instrument of avarice, employed for pecuniary gain instead of for the salvation of souls.[16] And the greedy ministers and agents make the poor victims believe that their soul bounds into heaven at the moment the money is paid.

But the deepest wound the Church has suffered from the clergy is their failure to preach the Word of God. Herein, he says, lies the basic cause of all the evil in the Church, including the indifference of the laity and the general deadness of the congregations. Priests and prelates are only men, and so they will occasionally fall into sin, even gross sin. But much greater is their guilt in failing to preach the Word. For then, as he tells his friend, the Provost of Leitzkau, in 1516, they not only sin as men, but they sin against their office.[17] So if they are perfectly holy in every way, but fail to preach the Word, they are not shepherds, but wolves.[18]

Luther is not in revolt against the Church and the ecclesiastical status quo. He has no patience with schismatics or heretics. The remedy for the corruption and the distress in the Church is not to go out of the Church and cause schism. There is only one remedy, it is the preaching of the Word. Consciously or unconsciously, the Reformer is speaking. Had the Leitzkau Sermon been preached in 1512, as was long assumed, Jundt would probably have been correct in saying that in it Luther for

---

[16] W. I, 65, L. 9.
[17] *Sermo . . . in praescriptis praeposito in Litzska in illud Joannis.* W. I, 12-13.
[18] *Loc. cit.*

the first time speaks as Reformer.[19] If it was preached in or about 1516 as the latest research finds, it is still true that it sounds one of the earliest trumpet calls to reform that we have from Luther. But the voice has already been heard in the "Lectures on the Psalms" of 1513-1516. The prophetic fact stands out that he so early put his finger on the very heart of the Church's ailment: the Word of God was not being preached. Do not these stupid priests know that the Word of God is the very life blood of the Church? "The idea is firmly established," he says in the Leitzkau Sermon, "that the Church is not born, nor does it subsist, in its own nature, except by the Word of God. 'He begat us by the Word of truth.' Just as the blessed virgin was the womb whence proceeded the Lord Christ, so Scripture is the womb whence spring divine truth and the Church."[20]

Already Luther is proclaiming another Scriptural truth that will soon become one of the pillars of the Reformation. The Word is the very foundation of the Church. In explaining Ps. 103 (104):24, he declares, "The Church is built on the Word of the Gospel, which is the Word of divine wisdom and virtue: just as the world, too, is visible, created from the beginning in the word and wisdom of God."[21] The Word gives birth to the Church, and the Word alone preserves and blesses it. This blessing, spoken of in Ps. 44 (45):4, signifies multiplication and growth. Since the grace on the lips of Christ is vast, so there follows a multiplication of the faithful, and this even in eternity, for the Church will never cease.[22] The "Word" is understood by Luther to mean

---
[19] Jundt, *Op. cit.*, p. 115.
[20] Ps. 70 (71), 6, W. III, 454, L. 24.
[21] W. IV, 189, L. 33.
[22] W. III, 259, L. 18.

primarily the holy Gospel. For the Gospel is complete and perfect; it is the judgment and the justice by which Christ rules His Church.[23] Its power is great, for it is the iron rod of Ps. 2:9, which is the regal scepter of Christ in His Church and Kingdom. It is called a rod, because it directs, affirms, rebukes, and protects.[24] It is Christ who wields this scepter, for He is the King of all power in the Church,[25] which is His Kingdom.[26]

The way Luther thus mixes up a scorching attack on the abuses in the Church with a positive application of the remedy presents him to us already, not as a rabid iconoclast, but as a constructive critic. Isn't that, after all, the last stepping stone in the making of a Reformer? And still Luther remains the faithful son of the Church. The corruption, the false doctrine, the desiccated preaching—he never suspects that it all comes from the system, the institution. It is only individual error. Straying already from the doctrinal bosom of the Roman Catholic Church, whether it be in the realm of justification or ecclesiology, he seems utterly unconscious of the fact which later years revealed so plainly. In all the works of the period we find him defending vigorously the authority and ordinances of the Church. Heresy is anathema, schism is spiritual suicide. But now we can see in due perspective how, with the growing polemic against error in the Church, there is developing in him a definite doctrine of the Church. Without any conscious effort to formulate it, as far as we can see, he nevertheless throws out statements here and there which show clearly that

---

[23] Ps. 71 (72), 4. W. III, 463, L. 22.
[24] W. III, 32, L. 2.
[25] Ps. 67 (68), 13. W. III, 394, L. 12.
[26] Ps. 44 (45), 7. W. III, 251, L. 5.

the doctrine is formulating itself in his thinking, even as his basic doctrine of justification is taking shape.

The real issue before us is "the Nature of the Church." And it is amazing to read the "Lectures on the Psalms" and see how far Luther has advanced already toward a complete doctrine of the Church. We noticed above how in Pss. 44 and 67 he called the Church the Kingdom of Christ. Now, in Ps. 88, he goes farther and discusses the nature of this Kingdom. It is not a bodily, earthly kingdom, but a spiritual kingdom. Luther compares the Church to the Old Testament Synagog and sees them both reflected in the death and resurrection of Christ. They dishonored, destroyed, and killed Christ according to His manhood. Thereby was symbolized that the whole body of the Synagog according to the flesh must be raised again into an immortal body. As Christ went from this life through death to another life, so He wished that the Law and the Synagog should go over from the life of the letter—transitory and visible—to invisible spirit and to an eternal Church through the destruction and death of the letter, shadows, and figures.[27] If the Church thus is a spiritual body, it must of necessity be *invisible*.

Karl Holl tells us at this point that the whole discussion about whether Luther knew the term "invisible Church," was from the beginning vain. And yet this very conflict of scholars makes it important to let Luther himself speak. "Invisible Church" does not appear very often in Luther. Much oftener he uses the term "spiritual Church" in the same sense.[28]

But if the Church is "spiritual" and "invisible," how

---
[27] Ps. 88 (89), 45. W. IV, 47, L. 21.
[28] Holl, *Op. cit.*, v. 1, p. 296, note 3.

do we know that it is present, and how can we share in its blessings? The answer is twofold. (1) The Church can be perceived only through the eyes of faith. "Invisible, perceptible through faith is the Church."[29] Seeberg seems to have overlooked this early statement of Luther. For he says that Luther first calls the Church invisible in his "Responsio ad Librum Ambrosii Catharini," a work from 1521.[30] We read the same arresting declaration in Ps. 91, where Luther says that the work of Christ in the Church, yea, the very structure itself, is invisible and cannot be seen except through spiritual eyes and faith.[31] Thus it is not in essence a visible body, but a spiritual communion,[32] bound together by a common faith.

We can see what Luther is coming to in this language. He is already arriving at a clear-cut conception of the Church as the "communion of the faithful." In fact the phrase occurs more than once in this period. In an early work of unknown date, the "Tractatulus de his, qui ad Ecclesias confugiunt," he speaks of the Church as the "communio fidelium,"[33] communion of the faithful. In Ps. 67 he compares the church member to Benjamin. "He who remains in the churches and the communion of saints is Benjamin."[34] Here we meet the term "communion of saints," which at this time begins to dominate Luther's thinking on this question. Again and again we meet it in the Psalms. "Thence is the communion of saints. One faith, one Lord, one Church," he says on

---

[29] Ps. 103 (104), 13. W. IV, 189, L. 17.
[30] *Studien zur Geschichte des Begriffes der Kirche*, p. 91, note 2. Erlangen: Deichert, 1885.
[31] W. IV, 81, L. 12.
[32] Ps. 110 (111), 1. W. IV, 239, L. 23.
[33] W. I, 4, L. 3.
[34] W. III, 406, L. 10.

Ps. 119:63.³⁵ It is plain that Luther has come to experience the glorious fellowship of the saints which is his in the Church, when he says, "Notice, that properly you ought so to pray this and all the Psalms together with all the faithful devoutly praying them, that it is evident that you wish your prayer to come before God with them and in the union and communion of saints."³⁶ The heretics are outside of this communion. They "shall not dwell within my house,"³⁷ says Ps. 100 (101):7. That means that they are not "on the inside, in the spirit, in the unity, in the bond of the communion of saints."³⁸

Here Luther has taken the ancient concept of the Communion of Saints and given it new meaning. He has extricated it from the traditional identity with the Roman Catholic Church and set it free to realize its full Scriptural meaning. For here was a spiritual community, subsisting by the Word and characterized by the faith and personal communion of the Christian with God and other Christians. That does not leave any Christian a lonely soul without friends or kin. For he belongs to a society far more intimate and compact than the visible Catholic Church. They, and they alone, compose the true Church, which is the mystical Body of Christ.³⁹

We come back to the question: If the Church is "spiritual" and "invisible," then how can we know that it is present? The first part of the answer was that the Church can be perceived only by faith.

The second part of the answer is that where the *Word*

---
³⁵W. IV, 289, Gl. 2, L. 25; cf. Ps. 32 (33), 7. W. III, 183, L. 20: "sanctorum congregatio."
³⁶Ps. 142, 1. W. LV, 443, Gl. 1, L. 26.
³⁷W. IV, 138, L. 30.
³⁸*Ibid.*, L. 33.
³⁹Ps. 31 (32), 1, W. III, 174, L. 25; Ps. 17 (18), 7. W. III, 113, Gl. 5, L. 19.

is preached, there is the Church. For the Word is never preached without bearing fruit.[40] This fruit is the "blessing" already mentioned, which consists in multiplication and growth.[41] And here comes an early reference to the question that troubles us most of all, the relation between the visible and the invisible in the Church. The preached Word does not reach all the hearers to win them. Some are won, some reject it.[42] These together form the *visible outward Church* where the good and bad are mingled together. This Luther does not himself call specifically the visible outward Church. He calls it the "congregation," in contrast with the "assembly of the upright." The Psalm in the first verse says, "I will praise the Lord with my whole heart, in the assembly of the upright, and in the congregation." The "assembly of the upright" Luther takes as the true Church, the communion of believers. The "congregation" he regards as the outward assembly of good and bad.[43]

But now he says that the "assembly of the upright" cannot exist except in the "congregation," wherein are mixed the wicked with the good. And one does not desert the congregation just because they are not all of the assembly of the upright. The vital thing, however, is that it is of little value, yea, it is nothing at all, to be in the congregation, if one is not in the assembly of the just. Therefore the Psalmist mentions first and foremost the assembly of the righteous, and thereafter the congregation. "Thus the sense is: I wish to be in Thy Church both in spirit and in body, both in merit and in number. For

---
[40]Ps. 44. W. III, 258, L. 38; 259, L. 15.
[41]Ps. 44, 4. W. III, 250, L. 18.
[42]Ps. 84 (85), 9. W. IV, 10, L. 22.
[43]Ps. 110 (111), 1. W. IV, 239, L. 22ff.

whoever is in the Church only in number, without merit, he is only in the congregation."[44]

This does not mean that a man can stand outside the congregation and say, "I belong to the assembly of the upright, I don't need to belong to the congregation." That attitude, which every pastor faces from time to time, Luther answers unequivocally in this lecture. He declares, "A person can be in the outward congregation and not in the assembly of the upright, *but he cannot be in the assembly of the upright and not be in the congregation.* Thus as wheat is not without chaff in the field, so there is no assembly of the upright except in the congregation. For the congregation is that mass from which men are chosen and adopted into the assembly of the upright and transferred from the number category to the merit. For if you take away that mass (congregatio), whence will the assembly of the upright be formed? Forsooth will it not perish? Therefore the two must be together."[45]

So far Luther had come through the study of the Psalms, even before the indulgence controversy. He already has a clear grasp of the Church as an invisible spiritual communion of believers, which is the Body of Christ. What a contrast to the visible, organized Church wherein he saw corruption and abuses on every hand! Not only were the clergy corrupt, but worst of all, they did not preach the Word which they were sent to preach, which was the very life-blood of the Church.

Scathing as was his attack on these abuses, it is still apparent that he never dreamed of revolt against the hierarchy at this time. On the contrary, he did not cease to condemn schism and to urge all men to obey the Church

---
[44] *Ibid.*, 240, L. 5ff.
[45] "Ergo simul oportet esse hec duo," *Ibid.*, L. 24-25. Cf. Ps. 48 (49), 6. W. III, 274, L. 17; Gl. 2, p. 273, L. 33; p. 632, L. 7.

and its appointed prelates. For the sake of order, authority and ordinances in the Church ought to be obeyed and respected. For the Catholic Church remained the God-appointed dispenser of the Word of Truth.

It was this Word, as Holl rightly points out, that gave Luther the link between the invisible spiritual Church and the so-called visible Church.[46] Since it is the Word by which the Church is born and preserved, there must be an agent charged with dispensing this Word. This agent was the institution with prelates holding the offices divinely ordained for the preaching of the Word.[47] That, to Luther at this stage, was the Catholic Church, to which every Christian should belong. He does not mince words when he tells the people, "Good works ought to be done under a prelate and in the unity of the churches, not in sects, heresies, and superstitions."[48] For "outside of the Church no confession can please God."[49]

There was just one ugly question waiting to raise its head to smash that comfortable argument to bits. It was the question that Luther had apparently not yet faced. When he did, he found himself at the crossroads and the parting of the ways with the hierarchy. What would happen if the prelates ceased to preach the Word of God entirely and the Church no longer taught in agreement with the Word? We do not find the answer in this period of Luther's development. Only here and there comes the suggestion of the doctrine of the spiritual priesthood of believers, which was later to play such an important role in his thinking.[50] For the present, however, it appears, as

---

[46] Holl, *Op. cit.*, v. 1, p. 304.
[47] Ps. 37 (38), 12. W. III, 217, L. 22.
[48] Ps. 103 (104), 17. W. IV, 186, 23, L. 23.
[49] Ps. 110 (111). W. IV, 239, L. 21.
[50] Ps. 108 (109), 8. W. IV, 224, L. 21: "Nam omnes fideles per Christum sacerdotem sunt sacerdotes et reges." Cf. Ps. 115 (116), 11. W. IV, 267, L. 17.

Strohl puts it, "he does not yet draw any conclusion from the principle of the universal priesthood."[51]

LECTURES ON ROMANS (1515-1516)

Luther's "Lectures on Romans" have little to contribute to our problem beyond what we found in the "Psalms."[52] This is not true of his theological development in general. Plunging now into the great Epistle, he not only interprets it but, as Hausrath so forcibly says, he "lives it." St. Paul's struggles are his struggles. "O wretched man that I am, who shall deliver me?" But finding the glorious comfort of the central truth of justification by faith, he sings, "Then was I glad. . . . The entire Holy Scripture and heaven itself were opened to me."[53]

Augustine, too, has lived the Epistle, he discovers, and so he regards him as Paul's greatest interpreter. German mysticism undoubtedly plays its part in Luther's development also. That may account for the "subjective" note which Grisar finds so prevalent in his work on Luther.[54] Is it possible that Grisar confuses subjectivism with a growing independence of church authority? For one does sense here that Luther is beginning to doubt the claim that the soul's only approach to God is through the Roman Church as intermediary. Not that he shows the slightest tendency to revolt. But he has discovered the sweetness of personal communion with God, and that discovery is bound to give a certain degree of spiritual independence. History tells us that this was to develop into a conception of Christian liberty which was alto-

---
[51] *L'Epanouissement de la Pensée religieuse de Luther de 1515 à 1520*, p. 293. Strassbourg, Paris: Libraire Itra, 1924.
[52] Holl. *Op. cit.*, Vol. I, p. 306.
[53] Adolf Hausrath, *Luthers Leben*, Vol. I, pp. 134-135. Berlin: Grote, 1905.
[54] Grisar. *Op cit.*, p. 180.

gether incompatible with hierarchical claims of absolute authority over the individual conscience. As yet, however, he raises no voice in protest against ecclesiastical authority. He still preaches obedience to the established order.

But in these "Lectures" he really lets himself go in a furious tirade against the corruption that he sees more plainly every day. The monks and priests are blind with avarice.[55] The Roman Curia is rotten as ancient Rome.[56] Pope and prelates have turned indulgences into a money-making racket.[57] The people are corrupted by ignorant preachers who tell fables instead of preaching the Word.[58]

These attacks, like those in the Psalms, never are turned from the individual upon the Church. The Church and its offices merit obedience, in spite of the corruption of the office-holders. The power lies, not in the heart of the preacher, but in the Word itself. Schismatics and heretics have no excuse. Their revolt against the Church is both stupid and selfish.[59]

But is there no remedy for the corruption that is ever on the increase? Yes, the duty of reforming and purifying the Church is ever present. But this is the duty, not of the laity, but of the duly ordained servants of the Church. It is for that reason that Luther feels himself more and more called on to raise his voice in protest. For he holds his teaching office by apostolic authority.[60] It is this feeling of responsibility, this distress of soul for himself and others, that finally drives him to the first great step of the Reformation, the posting of the "95 Theses."

---

[55] *Luthers Vorlesung über den Römerbrief 1515-1516;* hrsg. von Johannes Ficker. 4. aufl. Vol. II, p. 301, L. 23. Leipzig: Dieterich, 1930.
[56] *Ibid.*, p. 310, L. 8.
[57] *Ibid.*, p. 243, L. 16.
[58] *Ibid.*, L. 14.
[59] *Ibid.*, p. 238, L. 28; p. 334, L. 9.
[60] *Ibid.*, p. 301, L. 16; quia authoritate apostolica officio docendi fungor.

CHAPTER FIVE

Luther THE REBEL

In the face of Luther's consistent doctrinal development as we have seen it in his Lectures on the Psalms and Romans, it seems pathetic that an adversary should try to impugn his motives, as Grisar does at this point. This Roman Catholic writer poses the question why Luther felt called upon to formulate a new doctrine of the Church, new in contrast to the prevalent doctrine. Was it the natural consequence of his doctrinal development, or was he driven to it to justify his break with Rome? Grisar chooses the latter with an ingenious theory to bolster his argument. Luther, he says, had held his false doctrine of justification, with similar errors, a long time without a thought of separation from the Church or of questioning her traditional doctrines. Only when he saw that the Catholic Church would not adopt his new doctrine, but rather condemned it summarily, did he decide to tear himself loose from the Mother Church. To justify this step before his own conscience and to cover it up before the outside world, he proceeded to develop his theories concerning the nature of the Church.[1]

To arrive at this conclusion Grisar had to find that Luther's new idea of the Church first appeared in his

---
[1] Grisar. *Op. cit.*, Vol. III, p. 775.

sermon of 1518 on the virtue of the Papal ban.[2] Had that been true, Grisar's charge might have merited serious consideration. But Grisar has unfortunately overlooked the all-important "Lectures on the Psalms," where anyone can see, as we have seen, that Luther even between 1513 and 1516 laid a solid foundation for his doctrine of the Church and revealed that doctrine in all its elements.

THE INDULGENCE CONTROVERSY

The indulgence controversy does not contribute a great deal to our discussion. Luther here is so busy fighting, writing, debating, and defending himself against hostile attacks, that he has no time to concentrate on any formal definition of the nature of the Church. Nevertheless the period from the "95 Theses" to and including the "Leipzig Disputation" was a vital season of preparation, because Luther was compelled to analyze his relation to the authority of the Roman Catholic Church.

That question seems hardly to have entered his mind when he posted his "95 Theses." They were not meant to be an attack on the Church or the Papacy. It was an invitation to discussion, published in the usual way, and an attempt to bring to light the abuses in the Church. But the "Theses" were not received in that spirit. One after another, the heresy-hunting champions of Rome level their guns at him: Tetzel, Cajetan, Prierias, and Eck, in rapid succession. When they are through with him, the humble and obedient servant of Rome at Wittenberg has become the rebel of Leipzig, who dares to challenge the authority of the Roman Church, with its claims of the divine right of the Papacy and the infallibility of a General Council.

---

[2]*Sermo de virtute excommunicationis.* W. I, 634.

We cannot pass by the "95 Theses" altogether, because even Tetzel, in his Theses answering Luther's, regards the latter's theory of indulgences as springing from an erroneous conception of the Church, Papacy, and Council.³ And it is plain to us now that while Luther in the "Theses" was concerned with indulgences, nevertheless, before he was through defending them he saw that behind them lay, not only his doctrine of justification, but his conception of the Church.⁴

The first clash brought on by the "95 Theses" was on the Roman doctrine of the Treasure of the Church, or the Treasury of Merits. Christ had earned more merit than was necessary to atone for the sins of the world. The saints had done more than the Law required for their own salvation. So these superfluous merits lie there as a treasure of the Church. Out of it the Pope, as head of the Church, can grant indulgences.

Luther, debating with Prierias, Eck, and Cajetan, does not deny that Christ is the treasure of the Church. But He is not the treasure of indulgences. And these merits of Christ are available to the sinner without obtaining indulgence from the Pope or any other indulgence-vendor.⁵

Cajetan, meeting Luther at Augsburg in October, 1518, is quick to confront Luther with the fact that he has challenged a Papal decree, the "Extravagans," "Unigenitus," of Clement VI. Luther refuses to recant, because he places Scripture higher than any other author-

---
³*Secunda Disputatio Johannis Tetzelli.* Op. var. arg. I, 306-307.
⁴Holl. *Op. cit.*, Vol. I, p. 310; Th. Kolde, *Luthers Stellung zu Concil und Kirche*, p. 14. Gutersloh: Bertelsman, 1876.
⁵Thesis 58; also Resolutiones in W. Köhler, *Luthers 95 Thesen sammt seinen Resolutionen*, p. 163. Leipzig, 1903.

ity.⁶ That was the spirit of the 62nd Thesis, which rang clear and true with the declaration, "The true treasure of the Church is the most holy Gospel of the glory and the grace of God." Why should innocent people be persuaded to pass by that divine treasure for the empty treasure of indulgences?

Like the theme in a Wagnerian opera, sounds the note, louder and louder, that God rules the Church by His Word. The Church's power and authority lie not in ecclesiastical ordinances and offices but in the Word of God. As the importance of the Word grows in Luther's thinking on the Church, the importance of ecclesiastical powers and personages diminishes. The Church is a spiritual communion of believers, where Christ rules by His blessed Gospel.

This question would quickly draw us deeply into the realm of church polity and discipline. We pause only because here Luther makes his point clear, that the Keys were given to the Communion of Saints, to be administered wherever that is present through the administration of Word and Sacraments. Hence the Lord's Word to St. Peter in Matt. 16:18 cannot be used to bolster the power of Rome and the Papacy.

Luther discusses this matter in his "Resolutio super Propositione XIII" of 1519. The Keys were given to the Church alone, the Body of Christ, one flesh, living in the same spirit with Christ. The Church is the Peter who hears the revelation and receives the Keys. For here the Symbol stands firm, "I believe in the holy Church, the communion of saints"; not as some dream: "I believe the holy Church to be a prelate." "The whole world con-

---

⁶*Acta . . . Lutheri apud . . . Caietanum.* Op. var. arg. II, 369f.

fesses that it believes the holy catholic Church to be nothing else than the Communion of Saints." Hence, as the original Symbol did not have these words, "sanctorum communionem," they were added later to explain that the holy catholic Church is the "communion of saints."[7]

If this is true, then Pope and priest use the Keys only as servants of the Church, from which they receive them.[8] And as for the sinner, suffering under the burden of sin, he can receive the blessing of the Keys only within the Church. Luther's "Sermon von dem Sakrament der Busze" of 1519[9] gives the Gospel, or forgiveness, side of the power of the Keys.

But the Church also has power to "bind" sins upon one. This Luther explains in another sermon of earlier date, his "Sermo de Virtute Excommunicationis," delivered in the spring of 1518.[10]

This Sermon on Excommunication is important in the development of his doctrine of the Church. For here he reveals the comfort of the doctrine that the Church is not an organization which can condemn your soul to hell, but a spiritual communion of believers, into which only God can bring you and out of which only He can drive you. This was a vital matter to the many troubled consciences, smitten perhaps innocently by the excommunicating rod of the Church. How vital it must have been to Luther just now, when he surely must have seen that he was courting excommunication by his fearless attack on clergy and curia.

Here it is, as Luther must soon face it. The visible

---
[7] W. II, 189-190.
[8] *Ibid.*, 192.
[9] "Sermon on the Sacrament of Penance." W. II, 714-723.
[10] W, I. 638.

Roman Church can threaten, but he will take refuge in the arms of the invisible communion of all believers. There is a twofold communion of the faithful, he declares in this great sermon. There is an internal and spiritual communion of one faith, one hope, one love toward God. There is also an external and physical communion, a participation in the same Sacraments, that is, in the signs of faith, hope, and charity, which extends even to community of property, dwelling, etc.[11] No one but God, who brought you into the former, spiritual communion, can exclude you from it. In other words it is nothing but your own sin that excludes you.

The conclusion is that ecclesiastical excommunication is only a privation of external fellowship, of Sacraments, burial, and other bodily needs.[12] And it should be used as a gracious maternal rod, not to drive into hell, but to bring to repentance and to save.[13] Therefore it should be heeded and received with patience.[14]

This is Luther's comforting doctrine of the Church in action. If a soul is tyrannized by any external ecclesiastical organization, he can flee for comfort and consolation to the Communion of Saints and the spiritual fellowship which is in the common faith in Christ Jesus.

Luther throws himself into the indulgence controversy as a faithful son of the Church. He directs stinging attacks at the clergy, the Pope, the theologians, even the laggard laity. But his desire is only reformation in the Church. However, his sincerity was not appreciated, and his naiveté was soon jolted into painful sensibility of the terrible truth. The doctrines and practices that he was

---
[11] *Ibid.*, 639, L. 1.
[12] *Ibid.*, L. 9.
[13] *Ibid.*, L. 130.
[14] *Ibid.*, 643, L. 1ff.

attacking were not mere mistakes of erring individuals. They were, he began to see, the teachings and practices of the Roman Catholic Church, sanctioned by Rome itself. As the controversy progresses, the gulf between Luther and the established Church widens, until the crack of Wittenberg becomes the chasm of Leipzig.

Now he cannot escape the crucial issue. Duty has driven him to attack individual abuses and errors. But does he dare to question the established authority of the Church? How far may individual liberty of conscience and reason challenge ecclesiastical authority? May the individual approach God or interpret Scripture without the mediation of the Roman Church?

Luther is changing quickly now, in his attitude toward the Roman authority. In July, 1518, in the "Decem Praecepta," he pushes aside the nasty question, and says obediently, "He that trusteth in his own heart is a fool, and the Church *cannot err*."[15] It is a long jump from that position to the one he finally took at Leipzig, that a Council could err, and had erred. And in between those two points comes his admission that even the Pope is only a man and his opinion "moves me not at all," as he said in the "Resolutiones."[16]

It was Tetzel who first drew Luther out on the question of the Papacy. That was not the subject of Luther's "95 Theses." But Tetzel answers them with 50 Theses extolling the Papacy. His only purpose appears to have been to discredit Luther in the eyes of the Pope and the whole Church. At least it brought Luther face to face with the implications of his bold step. He was challenging the Church's claim to sole mediation between man

---
[15]The Ten Commandments. W. I, 444, L. 14.
[16]Resolutiones. W. I, 582; Aug. 1518.

and God. It was the advance pronouncement of the principle of individual liberty of conscience.

Eck joins in the fray with his "Obelisci" which Luther answers with the "Asterisci," both appearing in March, 1518.[17] Here Luther moves on and begins to question the Papal decretals, even while he is urging obedience to the Church.

This obedience to the Church is sincere. Luther loves his Holy Mother and yearns for her comforting support. He pours out his reverence for the Church in a beautiful sermon on Maundy Thursday, 1518. Let him who is weak in faith permit himself to be carried as a child in the arms and bosom of the Mother Church, even as the paralytic on his bed, that the Lord may at least regard her faith. Let him go in the faith of the universal Church, or of some faithful member, praying the Lord to accept him in the faith of his Church or of this or that member. For it is necessary to obey the Church which bids him draw near. And there is no doubt that God accepts obedience to the Church as obedience to Himself. Surely the faith of the Church will never allow him to perish.[18] Thus Luther desires the mediation of the Church and still cherishes her as his loving Mother.

As if he were afraid that he had offended the Pope, Luther in August, 1518, addresses his "Resolutiones" to the Pope. Putting himself in complete subjection to the Papal power he writes, "Wherefore, most blessed Father, I prostrate myself at your feet, with all that I am and possess: quicken, kill, call, revoke, approve, reprove, as you wish. I will acknowledge your voice as the voice of

---
[17]*Obelisks* and *Asterisks*. W. I, 278.
[18]*Sermo de digna praeparatione cordis pro suscipiendo Sacramento Eucharistiae*. W. I, 333. L. 13ff.

Christ, directing you and speaking in you. If I have deserved death, I refuse not to die."[19]

This note of submission is hardly in harmony with the rest of the work. The Roman Church is only a manmade institution, and its primacy is an artificial one, never acknowledged up to the time of Gregory.[20] He will heed the Pope when he speaks "as Pope," in the canons and according to the canons or a council, but not when he speaks according to his own head.[21]

It becomes clear in the same "Resolutiones" that Luther's awe of the Papacy is waning. And there emerges the opinion that the Pope is not the highest tribunal in the Church. This position is reserved for a General Council. The Pope has fallen before the authority of Scripture. What of a General Council?

It was Sylvester Prierias who extracted this from Luther, and made him say that a "Council can err."[22] Luther's "Responsio" to Prierias takes a step beyond the "Resolutiones." In the latter a Council is given an exalted position at the expense of the Pope. In the "Responsio" Luther is driven by Prierias to make the bold statement that Pope as well as Council *can* err.[23]

There is only one step more to take, that is to assert that a Council *has* erred. It was not till he was challenged by the browbeating Eck that Luther made that assertion. First, however, we find him at Augsburg, asserting to Cajetan the liberty of individual conscience and reason.[24]

---
[19] *Dr. Martin Luthers Briefwechsel*, bearb. von E. L. Enders, Vol. I, pp. 200-203. Frankfurt: 1884-1903. In a milder form in W. I, 527ff.
[20] W. I, 571.
[21] *Ibid.*, 582, L. 19.
[22] *Dialogus . . . de Potestate Papae*. Aug. 31, 1518. Op. var. arg. I, 341, and Luther's answer in *Ad Dialogum S. Prieritatis . . . Responsio.* W. I, 644.
[23] Op. var. arg. II, 22.
[24] Oct., 1518.

But at the same time he longs for peace, and goes so far as to say, "I respect and follow the holy Roman Church in all my words and deeds, present, past, and future. If anything has been said or will have been said to the contrary or otherwise, I wish it not to have been said."[25] In that spirit he begs Cajetan to submit the question to the Pope.

A month later, knowing that the Pope's thunder may peal at any moment, Luther appeals to a General Council on November 28, 1518.[26] It is apparent, as Dieckhoff points out, that Luther has finally discovered that the Pope is in the camp of his enemies.[27]

An interview with Miltitz early in 1519 seemed to have established a modus vivendi. In his "Unterricht auf Etliche Artikel"[28] Luther is prepared, he says, to keep quiet, only that he will exhort people to obedience to the Church. There was a lull. But with a crash comes Eck to fan the smoldering fire into flame again, and to drag Luther into a bitter struggle which ended with his break with ecclesiastical authority. Before it was over he had made up his mind on two matters: the head of the Church, and the authority of a Council.

Thus at the end of the indulgence controversy, the lonely warrior is still striving to preserve the unity of the Church, even while he is trying to cleanse it. But already, out of the controversy, there emerges in Luther a conception of the Communion of Saints which is quite different from the traditional one. The original idea of "communion" was not foreign to the Catholic. But it was

---

[25] *Acta . . . apud Dominum Legatum Apostolicum Thomam Caietanum Augustae.* Op. var. arg. II, 371ff.
[26] *Appelatio ad Consilium.* W. II, 36.
[27] *Der Ablaszstreit*, p. 227, 1886.
[28] W. II, 66.

spoiled by the note of self-seeking and merit which, running through all Catholic theology, necessarily colored also the doctrine of the Church. It is a modern Catholic theologian who has revealed the deep distinction between the Lutheran and the Roman conception. Scheeben-Atzberger, in his "Dogmatik" declares, "The Reformers did indeed let the article of faith concerning the Communion of Saints stand, but they emptied it of practically all of its content, in that they rejected many presuppositions to the Communion and most of the forms necessary for its realization (the existence of purgatory, the merit and satisfaction of good works, the holy Mass, the personal inner sanctification of man, the intercession of the saints, or at least the access to them in prayer)."[29]

Here the Catholic dogmatician betrays exactly the foreign and unscriptural elements which Luther felt had been added to the ancient tradition, and which must be driven out of their doctrinal system. These things were basic in Catholic thinking: merit, good works, human sufficiency. They must be replaced with grace, faith, and the all-sufficiency of the atonement of Jesus Christ. And here it becomes clear to us that there could be no Reformation until justification by faith was again the starting point of the Church's faith. Neither could there be any reformation in the doctrine of the Church until this basic factor had been cleared up. For into the doctrine of the Communion of Saints it brought the whole foreign idea of merit and self-seeking and personal profit. We are in the Church to *get* something more than to *give*. The saints have earned something for us, and we earn something for ourselves and for others. We have to reach up to those in heaven to get help, since the atonement of

---
[29]*Handbuch der Dogmatik*, Vol. IV, p. 882. St. Louis: Herder, 1878.

Christ is not ready and sufficient for us here below. This is too materialistic to satisfy the Scriptural idea that the Communion of Saints is one of love. And love is unselfish and seeks nothing beyond itself. Althaus is severe when he charges, that "through this self-seeking business of good works you will never attain to the Communion of Saints."[30]

Luther could set the idea of the Communion of Saints free from all this because God gave him grace to see that the sinner is justified by grace through faith in Jesus Christ. *Sola fides, sola gratia,* become also the foundation-stone of Luther's doctrine of the Church.

THE LEIPZIG DISPUTATION

In the 22nd conclusion of his "Resolutiones" Luther had asserted that before the time of Gregory I the Roman Church was not superior to other churches, at least not the Greek Church.[31] It was a distinct surprise to Luther when Eck, in the last of his "Thirteen Theses"[32] introducing the Leipzig Disputation, challenged this article. Luther answered in "Thirteen Theses,"[33] and in a larger work immediately following, enlarging on his 13th Thesis concerning the authority of the Pope and the Roman Church.[34] Here Luther is beginning to speak more bluntly and more courageously. "That the Roman Church is superior to all others is proved from the most valueless decrees of Roman Pontiffs, against which stand the text

---
[30]*Communio sanctorum.* (Forschungen zur Geschichte und Lehre der Protestantismus. 1. reihe, 1 bd.), p. 34. München: Kaiser, 1929.
[31]W. I, 571, L. 16.
[32]Walch XVIII, 860.
[33]*Contra novos et veteros errores . . . in studio Lipsensi.* Op. var. arg. III, 16
[34]*Resolutio Lutheriana Super Propositione XIII de Potestate Papae,* June, 1519. W. II, 180.

of divine Scripture, the approved histories of 1100 years, and the decrees of the most holy Nicene Council."[35]

Grant to both the Roman Church and her Pope a primacy of honor, even as Peter enjoyed among the apostles. But that does not give them any primacy of power, any more than Peter had such a primacy.

As concerns the Church, the universal and catholic Church existed long before the Roman Church.[36] And even Paul, in Rom. 15:25ff. makes it clear that he regards the Church at Jerusalem as the mother, the root and the source of all churches in the world, including the Roman Church.[37]

And as for the Pope, we give him a primacy of honor, and offer him obedience, because it is the will of God that we submit to human ordinances and government. The Papacy is such a man-made office, strengthened under God's disposition. But the adversaries cannot use the Scriptures to prove any primacy of power in that office. The Pope is a man like other bishops, and Luther will not accept his claim to infallibility and to the sole right of interpreting Scripture.[38] If the words "I will give unto thee the keys, etc." refer to the Pope and the Roman Church, then so do the words immediately following, "Get thee behind me, Satan."[39]

We recognize here a growing sense of individual liberty over against ecclesiastical authority. *Scripture* is what determines what is right. But this whole hierarchical structure, Papacy and all, is built on the flimsy fabric of *decretals*. The adversaries all say, It must be so, for the

---
[35]*Ibid.*, 185, L. 7
[36]*Ibid.*, 190, L. 27ff.
[37]*Ibid.*, 203, L. 28ff. Cf. p. 237, L. 23.
[38]*Ibid.*, 203, L. 28; 237, L. 23.
[39]*Ibid.*, 191, L. 21.

decretals say so. Luther says, It cannot be so, for Scripture says otherwise, when interpreted by Scripture and seen through the eyes of faith. The Church must be built on a more solid foundation than decretals. It must be built on the *faith* of its members. Faith is the essence of the Church, and where faith is, there is the church.[40] Therefore faith is the guiding principle of the individual, and he is no longer bound by the shackles of ecclesiastical authority. And so Luther repeats Augustine's principle, according to which every Pope must yield to the judgment of an individual believer, particularly in matters of faith.[41]

The crafty Dr. Eck has one purpose in view, to link Luther with the arch-heretics who preceded him. Wyclif said it was not necessary to salvation to believe that the Roman Church was supreme. Hus held that Peter was not the head of the Roman Catholic Church, and that the Papacy emanated from the Emperor. Marsilius asserted that Peter was no more head of the Church than the other Apostles. Now Eck wants to hear Luther's opinion as to these heretics.[42]

Luther calls it an affront to be labelled a friend of the Bohemians. He did not even know Hus's "De Ecclesia" at the beginning of the Leipzig Disputation. He says in a tract of 1520 that at the time of the Leipzig Disputation he had, alas, not read John, otherwise he "would have held, not only some, but all the articles condemned at Constance."[43] He has always been against schism, and always will be. The Bohemians do wrong to separate

---
[40] *Ibid.*, 209, L. 5; 208, L. 25.
[41] *Ibid.*, 205, L. 3.
[42] *Disputatio I. Eccii et M. Lutheri Lipsiae habita.* W. II, 275, L. 8.
[43] *Von den Neuen Eckischen Bullen und Lügen.* W. VI, 587.

themselves from the established authority and general unity, even though they have the divine right. But why does not someone "with fraternal charity refute their error to the glory of the Roman Church"?[44]

And these poor Bohemians. Why not admit that there is much good in what they say? Why have they been condemned for saying that there is one only universal Church, and that "it is not necessary to salvation to believe that the Roman Church is superior to all others"? Pity the poor Greek saints, who never held that article! If the Bohemians are heretics for not acknowledging the Pope, then so are a multitude of celebrated saints, whom the Church to this day honors as its greatest.[45]

Eck drives Luther on to the last ditch. If he defends the Bohemians, then he is attacking the celebrated Council of Constance. Luther at first says he has not spoken against the sacred Council, and does not desire to.[46] But he has questioned some of their decisions, and Eck says that means that they erred. Luther cannot contain himself any longer, and says outright, "I agree with the doctor, that in matters of faith the decrees of Councils ought to be esteemed in every way. This alone I reserve, which ought to be reserved, that a *Council occasionally has erred and can err*, at least in matters of faith. Nor does a Council have the authority to establish new articles of faith."[47]

With that statement of Luther, the last vestige of infallible authority disappears from a General Council, as

---
[44] *Von dem Papstthum zu Rom wider den hochberühmten Romanisten zu Leipzig.* W. VI, 278, L. 29.
[45] *Ibid.*, 279, L. 11.
[46] *Ibid.*, 283, L. 14.
[47] *Ibid.*, 303, L. 16.

far as divine right is concerned. In fact Luther had knocked the last prop of authority from under the Roman Church. If Pope and Council could err, and had erred, then what authority is left in the hierarchy? Luther knew the answer now. There was only one authority in the Church, that was the Word of God. From that alone Pope and Council could draw authority. On this foundation alone could the Church endure.

But the trembling followers of Luther must have been asking, "Will not the Church totter and fall when the old authorities, accepted for centuries, are literally swept away?" No lesser man than Erasmus saw the danger of that. The medieval conception of the Church had been shaken, and to many the Church of Christ seemed to hang in thin air, its foundation gone.

But Luther had not come to destroy, but to build. Even while he was engaged in demolishing the man-made authority of the hierarchy, his revived New Testament conception of the Church as a spiritual communion of believers was growing into a workable reality. The elements of the doctrine we have seen were present long before the conflict with Rome began. And yet the years of controversy were like a fertilizer, giving growth and strength to those fundamental principles. Having liberated himself from the shackles of traditional authority, Luther was free to collect these principles into a unified and complete doctrine of the Church.

CHAPTER SIX

THE *Communion* OF SAINTS

Luther's break with Roman ecclesiastical authority was complete at Leipzig. The subsequent papal bull and Luther's burning of the same were a mutual, formal recognition of the fact. From Leipzig he goes home to Wittenberg and takes up his pen. During the period leading up to Worms he reaches the height of his productivity. Treatises, tracts and sermons literally pour forth from his tireless pen. More than one of the works of the period are masterpieces of literary style. Their political significance is second only to their theological importance. It is evident that Luther feels he has cast off the bonds of ecclesiastical authority, for he writes with an abandon which bespeaks a conscience that is free and an intellect that is unfettered. The same circumstances give a new color to his works. The destructive note which necessarily predominated in his controversial writings gives way to a constructive one. He has destroyed, now he will build. The transition as far as our subject goes, appears in his great work of June, 1520, on "The Papacy at Rome."[1] Here he not only exposes the Roman doctrine of the Church to a devastating attack but on its very ruins

---

[1] *Von dem Papstthum zu Rom wider den hochberühmten Romanisten zu Leipzig*, 1520. W. VI, 277.

he builds his own Scriptural doctrine of the Church in its third and last stage.

"I welcome the opportunity," he says in the introduction, "to give the laity some explanation of the nature of the Church and to contradict the words of these seductive masters."[2]

With that introduction he proceeds to state the issue. "This, then, is the question: whether the papacy of Rome, possessing the actual power of all Christendom (as they say), is of divine or human origin; and this being decided, whether it is possible for Christians to say that all other Christians in the world are heretics and apostates, even if they agree with us in holding to the same Baptism, Sacrament, Gospel, and all the articles of faith . . . but merely do not have their priests and bishops confirmed by Rome . . . or, as it is now, buy such confirmation with money and let themselves be mocked and made fools of like the Germans."[3]

The issue appears to resemble that debated at Leipzig. Nevertheless we have already seen from Luther's introduction to the work, that he aims beyond a mere rehearsing of old arguments against the papacy. His purpose is to explain the true nature of the Church according to Scripture and to expose the false Roman doctrine of the Church. This he proceeds to do by presenting the two conceptions in contrast to one another. His opponent, Alveld, has given him the traditional Roman theory of the Church as the visible, outward Roman Catholic Church with its head at Rome. In answering Alveld's attack Luther presents his doctrine of the nature

---
[2](Meaning Prierias, Eck, Emser, etc., and their mouthpiece Albeld) *Ibid.*, 286, L. 24. Tr. by A. Steimle. Holman, I. 339.
[3]*Ibid.*, 286, L. 35. Holman, I. 340.

of the Church as the invisible, spiritual Communion of Saints.

Luther first disposes of the personal element in Alveld's attack. Meeting him with the same language Luther says: "I had not believed it possible to meet such dense, massive and stubborn error and ignorance in any man, much less in a saint of Leipzig. For the benefit therefore of this numskull, and of those led astray by him, I must first of all explain what is meant by these things—the Church, and the one Head of the Church."[4]

There is a question here about the use of the word Church, or "Kirche." We follow the translation in the Holman Edition throughout this work also in the rendering of the term "Christenheit." The translator comments on this word as follows: "Luther carefully avoids the use of the word 'church' (Kirche). The reason will appear in the argument which follows. In many places, however, the word 'Christendom' would not render Luther's meaning, and there is for the modern reader no such technical restriction to the term 'church' as obtained among Luther's readers."[5] Kattenbusch finds in Luther's usage "that after 1518 he develops a certain hesitancy toward the word 'Church' (Kirche). In the Latin he sticks to *ecclesia*. In the German he begins to prefer 'Christendom' (Christenheit). This is in harmony with the fact that he sees the 'two-sidedness' (Doppelschichtigkeit) of the matter."[6] This is a generalization favorable to Kattenbusch's thesis; but it is hardly substantiated by the evidence. The works which concern the Church, notably the response to

---
[4] *Ibid.*, 292, L. 29. Holman, I. 348-349.
[5] *The Papacy at Rome*. Holman, I. 339, note 2.
[6] F. Kattenbusch. "Die Doppelschichtigkeit in Luthers Kirchenbegriff." *Theologischen Studien und Kritiken* (Lutherana V), jhrg. 1927-28, 100 bd., 2-3. hft. p. 285.

Emser show no particular hesitation on Luther's part to employ the word *Kirche*

The conflict in the two conceptions is clear-cut. To Alveld the Church is the external, visible organization. To Luther it is the invisible, spiritual communion of believers. The unity of the Church to Alveld depends on outward membership in the Roman Catholic Church. To Luther it is a unity of faith in one Lord. While Alveld finds three uses for the word Church (Christenheit), Luther can find only one in Scripture. There the Church is called the assembly of all the believers in Christ upon earth, just as we pray in the Creed: I believe in the Holy Ghost, the Communion of Saints.[7] It is this spiritual Church which alone is the object of faith. No one says: "I believe in the Holy Ghost, one holy Roman Church, a communion of Romans."[8] This community consists of all those who live in true faith and love; "so that the essence, life and nature of the Church is not a bodily assembly, but an assembly of hearts in one faith, as St. Paul says, Ephesians 4: 'one baptism, one faith, one Lord.' "[9] Though far separated they constitute "an assembly in spirit because each one preaches, believes, hopes, loves, and lives like the other. So we sing of the Holy Ghost: 'Thou, who through divers tongues gatherest together the nations in the unity of the faith.' That means in reality a spiritual unity, because of which men are called a communion of saints. And this unity is of itself sufficient to make a Church, and without it no unity, be it of place, of time, of person, of work, or of whatever else, makes a church."[10]

---

[7]*Von dem Papstthum zu Rom.* W. VI, 292, L. 37. Holman, I. 349.
[8]*Ibid.*, 300, L. 34; H., I, 361.
[9]*Ibid.*, 293, L. 1. H., I, 349.
[10]*Ibid.*, 293, L. 5ff.

This spiritual *unity,* which alone "makes a church," is not *external* as the Romans make out. Christ's word to Pilate, "My kingdom is not of this world," clearly makes the Church (Christenheit) separate from all temporal communities and from anything external.[11] "And this blind Romanist makes of it an external community, like any other. Christ says even more clearly, Luke 17, 'The kingdom of God cometh not with observation: neither shall they say, Lo, here, or lo, there! for behold, the kingdom of God is within you.' "[12] The source of this perverted Romanist conception is a failure to study and understand Scripture. "I am astounded," Luther exclaims, "that such strong, clear words of Christ are treated as a joke by these Romanists, for by these words it is clear to everyone that the *kingdom of God* (for so He calls His Church) (Christenheit) is not at Rome, or here, or elsewhere. It is a nauseating lie, and Christ is made a liar when it is said that the Church is in Rome, or is bound to Rome—or even that the head and the authority are there by divine right."[13]

The *unity* of the Church is completely misunderstood by the Romanists when they make it a matter of external membership. It is a cruel error, "when the unity of the Christian Church (Christlichen Gemeyne), separated by Christ Himself from all material and temporal cities and places, and transferred to spiritual realms, is included by these preachers of dreams in material communities, which must of necessity be bound to localities and places. How is it possible . . . that spiritual unity and material unity

---
[11] *Ibid.,* L. 13ff.: "Das ist yhe ein klarer Spruch, damit die Christenheit wirt auszgetzogen von allen weltlicken Gemeynen, das sie nit leiplich sey."
[12] *Ibid.,* L. 16.
[13] *Ibid.,* L. 20.

should be one and the same?" Rome is deceiving the people in teaching that membership in the outward unity of the Roman Church places them in the spiritual unity of Christ's Church. For there are many "who are in the external assembly and unity, who yet by their sins exclude themselves from the inner spiritual unity. Therefore, whosoever maintains that an external assembly or an outward unity makes a church, sets forth arbitrarily what is merely his own opinion."

Luther finds that the Roman error always gets back to a misinterpretation of Scripture. Alveld and his Romanists make God and Scripture liars by explaining everything that is written concerning the Church (Christenheit) as meaning the outward show of Roman power. "And yet he cannot deny that the large majority of these people, particularly in Rome itself, because of unbelief and evil lies, is not in the *spiritual unity*, i.e., the true Church (Christenheit). For if to be in the external Roman *unity* made men true Christians, there would be no sinners among them, neither would they need faith nor the grace of God to make them Christians; this external unity would be enough."[14]

From this Luther draws his conclusions as to *who are the true members of the Church*. He declares that "just as being in the Roman unity does not make one a Christian, so being outside of that unity does not make one a heretic or un-Christian." External fellowship with the Roman Church Luther does not find to be commanded by divine law; hence it is not vital. "To be in this place or that, does not make a heretic; but to be without true faith makes a man a heretic." *Faith* is spiritual and in-

---

[14]*Ibid.*, 293, L. 35ff. Holman, I. 350.

visible, and mere outward membership in the Church does not reveal its presence. "To be a member of the Roman communion (Sammlung) does not mean to be in true faith, and to be outside of it does not mean to be in unbelief; otherwise those within it would all be believers and truly saved, for no one article of faith is believed without all the other articles. Therefore, all those who make the Christian communion a material and outward thing, like other communities, are in reality Jews (for the Jews likewise wait for their Messiah to establish an external kingdom at a certain definite place, namely, Jerusalem), and thus sacrifice the faith, which alone makes the kingdom of Christ a thing spiritual and of the heart."[15]

Extremely important for the understanding of Luther's conception of the Church is his discussion of it in terms of *body and soul*. Membership in the true Church, says Luther, is a matter not of the body but of the soul, that is, of faith. "As the body is a figure or image of the soul, so also the bodily community is a figure of this Christian spiritual community. If the Church (Christenheit) were a bodily assembly, you could tell by looking at the body whether anyone were Christian, Turk or Jew; just as you can tell by the body whether a person is a man, woman or child, or whether he is white or black. Again, I can tell whether one is gathered in temporal assembly with others in Leipzig, Wittenberg or elsewhere; but I cannot tell at all whether he is a believer or not. Whosoever would not go astray should therefore hold fast to this, that the Church (Christenheit) is a spiritual assembly of souls in one faith, and

---

[15]*Ibid.*, 294, L. 16ff. Holman, I. 352.

that no one is reckoned a Christian for his body's sake; in order that he may know that the true, real, right, essential Church (Christenheit) is a spiritual thing, and not anything external or outward, by whatever name it may be called." So to Luther membership in the Church is a spiritual thing, and nothing will make a man a Christian and a member of the Christian Church except faith. And again he drives home his authority: "It is in this wise, and never in any other, that the holy Scriptures speak of the holy Church and of Christendom."[16]

Contrary to this Scriptural conception, another has arisen. This gives the name Church (Christenheit) to an assembly in a house or a parish, a bishopric, or the Papacy, in which assembly external rites are in use. Violence is done to the words, "spiritual" and "Church" by applying them to priests and bishops, not on account of their faith, but on account of their ordination, duties, garb, etc. This misuse of terms has confused many souls and induced them to believe that such outward show is the spiritual and only true estate in Christendom or the Church.[17]

Luther challenges his opponent and the Romanists to produce one letter of Scripture to prove that theory of the Church, or to substantiate the claims of Rome, that the Roman Catholic Church is the one and only Church, apart from which there is no Church, visible or invisible. He could not possibly put it stronger than he does to Alveld: "There is not one letter in the holy Scriptures to show that such a purely external Church has been established by God."[18] The Church which the Romanists speak of is not the Church of Scripture. And so, for the

---
[16]*Ibid.*, 295, L. 25. Holman, I. 354—cf. Edinburgh Report.
[17]*Ibid.*, 296, L. 16. Holman, I. 345.
[18]*Ibid.*, Holman, I. 355.

sake of brevity, he will call the two churches by different names. "The first, which is the natural, essential, real and true one, let us call a spiritual, inner Christendom. The other, which is *man-made* and external, let us call a bodily, external Christendom: not as if we would part them asunder, but just as when I speak of a man, and call him, according to the soul, a spiritual, according to the body, a physical, man; the Apostle is wont to speak of the inner and of the outward man. Thus also the Christian assembly, according to the soul, is a communion (Gemeyne) of one accord in one faith although according to the body it cannot be assembled at one place, and yet every group is assembled in its own place."[19] This Christendom according to the body is composed of popes, cardinals, priests, and all who in external things are taken to be Christians, whether they are Christians at heart or not. Membership in this external body does not make them Christians, for it does not mean that they have faith. "Nevertheless this communion is never without some who at the same time are true Christians, just as the body does not give the soul its life, and yet the soul lives in the body and, indeed, can live without the body."[20]

---
[19] *Ibid.*, W. VI, 296, L. 30. Holman, I. 355.
[20] *Ibid.*, 297, L. 10. Holman, I. 355f.

CHAPTER SEVEN

THE OBJECT OF OUR *Faith*

It is evident that we are facing here the crux of our whole problem, the so-called question of the *visible and invisible Church*. It is the most difficult point of all. From Augustine down, theologians have wrestled with it and come to vague, conflicting conclusions. And when we consider that Luther had to tear himself loose from a conception which had been established and taken for granted for centuries by the whole Church, we can appreciate the difficulty of his task. Is there, perhaps, a mystery here that will never be solved? Is it, as Kohlmeyer declares, when he speaks of the relation between the "visible" and the "invisible" Church, "From the necessary transition of the Church to this outward appearance and from the conflict between these two arise the insoluble problems in Luther's thinking on the Church"?[1]

Luther, as we noted in a preceding paragraph, spoke in an unguarded moment of two churches. This has been one of the causes of confusion in the various interpretations of his conception of the Church. But he said distinctly that he did it only "for the sake of brevity" and to distinguish the organized Roman Church from the spiritual Communion of Saints. Alveld knows only the

---

[1] "Die Bedeutung der Kirche für Luther." *Zeitschrift für Theologie und Kirche*, 1928, Heft 4, p. 466.

first Church. Luther knows only the second. It is not true that Luther held there were two churches, one visible, the other invisible. The first one is not *the* Church. It is not even "established by God."[2]

Much confusion exists because this problem has not been discussed strictly within the sphere of the *nature* of the Church. If the question is approached from that angle, Luther's conception unfolds itself much more clearly. It at once becomes impossible to hold that Luther ever conceived of the Church as being, in essence, a visible body. The testimony of Luther himself is abundant to the effect that the Church in its very nature is invisible.

Luther speaks more specifically of the invisibility of the Church in two succeeding works written to Emser and Murner.[3] He contrasts their visible Roman Church with the invisible, spiritual Church of Scripture. The Church, he says, is not to be seen and found in a certain place. "All Christians in the world pray, 'I believe in the Holy Ghost, the holy Christian Church, the communion of saints.' If that article is true, then it follows that no one can *see or feel* the holy Christian Church, nor say, Lo, here; lo, there. For what one believes one does not see or find, as St. Paul teaches in Hebr. 11. Further, what one sees or feels one does not believe."[4]

In his crisp language he contrasts "the holy Church of Christ and the mad Church of the Pope."[5] "The holy Church of Christ says: 'I believe in a holy Christian Church.' The mad Church of the Pope says: 'I see a holy

---
[2] *The Papacy at Rome.* Holman, I. 355.
[3] *Auf das Überchristlich, Übergeistlich und Überkunstlich Buch Bocks Emsers zu Leipzig Antwort.* March, 1521. W. VII, 614.
[4] *Ibid.*, 684, L. 20ff.
[5] *Ibid.*, 685, L. 3.

Christian Church.' The former says: 'The Church is neither here nor there.' The latter says: 'The Church is here and there.' The former says: 'The Church rests on no person.' The latter says: 'The Church rests on the pope.' The former says: 'The Church is not built on a temporal foundation.' The latter says: 'The Church is built on the Pope.' " Is it not clear, then, that the Church cannot be pointed at, but only believed? In spite of Murner and all the Papists the Church is and will continue to be a spiritual city, invisible and in the Spirit, and built upon Christ Himself.

It is not strange that this assault on the very foundations of the medieval ecclesiastical structure should open a floodgate of opposition, not to mention personal abuse which was the order of the day in 16th century debating circles. Luther takes them as they come. And every time he utters his defense, his conception of the Church stands out more clearly. Ambrosius Catharinus argues in the traditional vein, defending the Roman position on the basis of Matt. 16. Luther answers that the Church of which Christ speaks there is the one true spiritual Church, built on Christ, the rock, and not on the Pope or the Roman Church. "Just as the rock is without sin, invisible and spiritual, so must the Church, which is without sin, be *invisible* and spiritual, to be *grasped* only *by faith.*"[6]

So far from being the "rock," the Pope is the "servant of the devil and the Pope's Church a school of the devil," while Christ, the Righteous One, is a king of righteousness and His Church the Communion of Saints.[7] And

---
[6] *Ad Librum eximii Magistri Nostri Magistri Ambrosii Catharini . . . Responsio M. Lutheri.* W. VII, 710, L. 1.
[7] *Ibid.,* 712, L. 37.

when we confess, "I believe in a holy Christian Church," we confess openly that the Church is *not visible,* for *faith* does not concern itself with what is visible.[8]

From all this it seems clear, in spite of all that some scholars have been able to offer to the contrary, that Luther knows only one Church, the invisible, spiritual Church, which is the communion of believers. He does not admit the distinction between a visible and an invisible Church, nor does he permit the statement that the Church is visible.[9] Certainly it is the Lord's will that Christians should gather together in congregations for prayer and worship and the administration of the Means of Grace. But the outward organization as to form is a man-made institution, indeed, built by men of God around the gifts of God, but—as we have already quoted Luther—"There is not one letter in the Holy Scriptures to show that such a purely external Church has been established by God. . . . The Canon Law and human statutes, indeed, give the name of Church, or Christendom, to such a thing, but that is not now before us."[10]

---

[8] *Ibid.,* 710, L. 4.
[9] Cf. J. T. Köstlin. *Luthers Lehre von der Kirche,* p. 107. Stuttgart: Liesching, 1853.
[10] *The Papacy at Rome.* Holman, I. 355.

We may agree with Sohm when he says, "Die geistliche Kirche erzeugt mit Notwendigkeit Versammlungen (denen heute diese, morgen andere angehören können), aber keine Körperschaft (keine rechtlich verfaszte Gemeinde)." In this he says Luther's position accords with that of the Early Church. In a preceding paragraph he intimates that Luther's position was not in accord with the Early Church. They felt they were the New Testament Israel and had not arrived at the grasp of the invisibility of God's people. Hence the Early Church became Catholic. And it all came from the old heathen idea of God's visible people. (Weltliches und geistliches Recht, p. 57. München und Leipzig: Duncker & Humblot, 1914.)

This incidental conclusion of Sohm is open to question. The New Testament, interpreting the Old, clearly distinguishes between the historical Israel and the spiritual Israel. "They are not all Israel, which are of Israel" (Rom. 9:6). Was not God's people the same to the early Christians as it was to Luther, viz., the body of true believers, known to God and found where Word and Sacraments are rightly administered?

But this does not mean that this communion or fellowship of believers is not something real and living and to be exercised in the life of the Church. Luther takes this spiritual conception of the Church and shows how realistic and practical it is in the Christian life in the Church: "Therefore it is also profitable and necessary that the love and fellowship of Christ and all saints be hidden, invisible and spiritual, and that only a bodily, visible and outward sign of it be given us. For were this love, fellowship and help known to all, like the temporal fellowship of men, we should not be strengthened nor trained thereby to put our trust in the invisible and eternal things, or to desire them, but should much rather be trained to put our trust only in the temporal, visible things and to become so accustomed to them as to be unwilling to let them go and to follow God onward; we should thus be prevented from ever coming to Him, if we followed God only so far as visible and tangible things led us. For everything of time and sense must fall away, and we must learn to do without them, if we are to come to God."[11]

Think of what a source of comfort this could be for the Church as it is in Germany and the other war-torn countries, where church buildings are destroyed, the outward organization smashed, leaders killed, and all ecclesiastical machinery gone to pot, to know that with the Gospel of Christ still living among them, there is still in the midst of them Jesus Christ and His Church, which is His Body. And the gates of hell shall not prevail against that Church. That gives contemporary significance to the comforting word of Luther when he says, in his Preface to the Apocalypse of St. John,

---

[11]*Ein sermon vom Sakrament des Leichnams Christi und von den Bruderschaften*, 1519. W. II, 752, L. 36. Holman, II. 24.

"Hence let offense, conspiracy, heresy and transgression come and do what they will; as long as the Word of the Gospel remains with us in purity and we hold it dear and precious, we shall not doubt that Christ is with us, even when things are at their worst."[12]

Through the maze of conflicting interpretations which scholars give to Luther's references to the Church we can find our way to a few basic conclusions drawn from the clear language of Luther himself.

1) The Church according to its nature is the Communion of Saints, the fellowship of believers, the Body of Christ, the Kingdom of God.

2) As such it is spiritual and invisible, perceptible only to faith.

3) This one Church manifests its presence on earth in assemblies of men where the Word is preached and the Sacraments administered according to the Word of God.

Some call this the visible Church. But that term is misleading. Are the visible and the invisible Church then identical? The answer is "No." For the "visible Church," so-called, has in it both believers and unbelievers, and no one can say which is which. Then that "visible Church" is not the Body of Christ. It is not the Communion of Saints and the fellowship of believers. But we must rather conclude that within that visible Church there exists the true Church, consisting of believers only. These believers constitute the Church, the Communion of Saints.

If then we persist in using the term visible Church, we must define our terms. This attempt has been made in many different ways. Some say the Church has taken on

---

[12]*Vorrede auf die Offenbarung S. Johannis*, 1545. Erlangen, LXIII, 168.

the form of a servant in this world.[13] The visible Church is only the *larva*, or mask, of the true Church.[14] Others speak, not of the visible Church, but of the visibility of the Church. For, says Rudolph Sohm, the administration of the Word, including Sacrament, is visible.[15] But whether we say the latter is visible or not, we must ask whether that makes the Church visible. For when the Word is preached, can anyone see that it is the Word of God? Is it not only faith that can recognize that it is the Word of God? Can the unbeliever tell whether it is a Christian or a Unitarian message, whether it is human philosophy or the true Word of God? Hence there, too, the presence of the Church, as well as the Church itself, is perceptible only to faith. Again and again we are thrown back upon our simple confession of faith, "I *believe* in the holy Christian Church, the Communion of Saints." And because I *believe* in it, believe that it is in truth the Body of Christ, and that by His grace I am a member of that Body, and that the gates of hell shall not prevail against it, and that in that Body I have the Word of life, therefore it is so unspeakably precious.

4) Finally, we have become aware that Luther has here uncovered again the ancient tradition of the Apostolic Church. What a contrast between this simple conception of the Church as the spiritual fellowship of believers in the Body of Christ, born and sustained by the Word and Sacraments, and the organized political monstrosity which is the hierarchy of Rome and which they call the Church!

---

[13]"Knechtgestalt." E. Kohlmeyer. *Op. cit.*, p. 502.

[14]*Loc. cit.* "Aber man darf bei dieser sichtbaren Kirche, wenn man ihr Wesen nicht völlig verzeichnen will, niemals eins vergessen, sie ist die Larva, mehr nicht."

[15]Rudolph Sohm, *Kirchenrecht*, Vol. I, p. 465. Leipzig: Duncker & Humblot, 1892-1923.

What does the New Testament know about an infallible Pope who is the vicar of Christ and the visible head of the Church on earth? Nothing. And it took 18 centuries for the barnacles of Roman traditions and errors to smother the true tradition so completely that the Vatican Council finally in 1870 dared to declare the infallibility of the Pope in ex cathedra pronouncements. In the same breath came the monstrous decree that "the Roman Pontiff possesses the primacy over the whole world"![16]

Take again that incriminating statement of the Roman dogmatician, Scheeben-Atzberger,[17] that the Reformation preserved the article of the Communion of Saints, but emptied it of practically all of its content. How did they empty it of its content? By rejecting the doctrines of purgatory, satisfactions, the merit-value of good works, the Mass, personal sanctification, intercession of the saints or the privilege of calling on them. Personal sanctification does not belong in that catalog, since Luther emphasizes that element more than Rome does, and, shall we say, both in theory and in life. But the rest of the catalog is correct. Luther rejected them all. And why not? Every one of them is foreign to the apostolic tradition, and is an accretion of later date. That, says Luther,[18] is not the Church which the New Testament gives us. And the burden of proof lies with Rome to prove that it is. If they cannot, then they thereby prove that they are not the Church and we are not heretics, as they call us. The issue is clear. One of us is the Church of Christ, the other is the church of the devil. But, says Luther, "what if I prove that we (and not Rome) have remained with the

---
[16]"Dogmatic Decrees of the Vatican Council." Schaff, Philip, *The Creeds of Christendom*, Vol. II, pp. 270-272. New York: Harper, 1877.
[17]Scheeben-Atzberger. *Op. cit.*, p. 882.
[18]*Wider Hans Worst*, 1541. W. LI, 477.

true ancient Church, yes, that we are the true ancient Church, and that you have separated from us, *i.e.,* from the ancient Church, and have erected a new church in conflict (wider) with the ancient Church?"[19]

With that salute, Luther launches into one of the most devastating indictments of the Roman Church that we have from his pen. He takes one doctrine at a time. He shows how he and his followers have maintained the ancient doctrine and thus remained faithful to the apostolic tradition. The Roman Church, on the other hand, has strayed from the tradition, changed it, added to it, and thus developed a doctrine which is entirely foreign to the original position of the Church. The Sacraments, the Keys, the Word, the preaching office, the "Our Father," the hymns, the divine institution of marriage, cross-bearing—in all these things Luther proves that he has remained faithful to the Scriptures and the apostolic tradition. He concludes the first part of his discourse with the challenge to Rome, "We have now proved that we are the true ancient Church, that we are one body with the entire holy Christian Church and one communion of saints. Now you Papists prove that you are the ancient true Church or equal to it. But that you cannot do, for I shall prove that you are the new false church, which is consistently unfaithful to the ancient true Church, yes, the devil's whore and school."[20]

From defense Luther then takes the offensive. In every one of these doctrines he shows how Rome has drifted from the original tradition and hence no longer represents the true Church in any sense. As an example of his treatment we can take his first point. To begin with, he

[19]*Ibid.,* 478-479.
[20]*Ibid.,* 487.

tells the Romanists, you do not abide by the first ancient Baptism. For you have added many other baptisms. The first Baptism is lost because of sin. And man must make satisfaction by his own works, particularly by the monastic way, through which a man is made as clean as if baptized by Christ. So they have filled the world with churches and monasteries.[21]

At this point Luther analyzes their basic error. He says that this matter of satisfaction is the beginning and the source and the door of all the abominations of the Papacy, even as Baptism is the beginning of, and entrance to, all grace and forgiveness. When there is no Baptism, there Sacrament, Keys, and all the rest profit nothing. And if the idea of satisfaction had not arisen, there would be no indulgences, pilgrimages, brotherhoods, Mass, purgatory, cloisters, with the many other abuses. Now, he says, show where in Scripture you find all this work-righteousness! Where do you find it in the ancient Church, since you dare to concoct such new ideas of Baptism and righteousness? And then follows the refrain which he repeats after every doctrine has been examined: "Who is the heretic, the schismatic, the new church?"[22]

What have the Romanists done to reach this state of confusion? They have put human traditions on equal basis with Scripture. For "the Pope is such an ass that he neither can nor will learn to distinguish between the Word of God and human teachings, but holds them both alike."[23] Thence comes this tragic situation, that every doctrine of the Roman Church is a confusion of divine Scripture and human tradition. Since to Rome they both

---
[21] *Loc. cit.*
[22] *Ibid.*, 487-488.
[23] *Ibid.*, 508.

stand on the same level of authority, it makes no difference how much there is of one and how much of another in their doctrinal statements. Here was another basic error of the new Pelagianism which Luther had to explode. Could he make Rome see that Scripture was the only source of doctrine and the final authority for faith and life, he would have kindled a fire which would have burned the whole vile structure of satisfactions and penances to ashes. And then the skeleton which was left would be the ancient apostolic tradition. That was the Reformation. Would to God that Rome had seen it!

CHAPTER EIGHT

THE *Perennial* REFORMATION

Luther's language in the preceding has lifted us above all the confusion of theological tongues, and left us with the clear principle that the Church is not visible to the eye, but only perceptible through faith. In other words, only a believer can know that the true Church is present. But even he must have some signs or evidence by which to recognize its presence. These signs, says Luther, are the Word and Sacraments. Baptism, the Bread, and above all the Gospel, "these three are the symbols, watchwords, and marks of Christians." Wherever these are found in whatever place, among whatever people, there we can be certain that the Church is.[1] For in these signs it is the will of Christ that we shall be one, as we read in Ephesians 4, "one faith, one baptism, one Lord." Where the same Gospel is, there is the same faith, the same hope, the same love, the same spirit and all truth. Now we understand better the "unity of spirit" which Luther emphasized so strongly. This is the unity of spirit which St. Paul bids us preserve so jealously, which is not a unity of place, of

---

[1] *Ad . . . Ambrosii Catharini.* W. VII, 720, L. 32ff.

person, of property or of bodies.² That is what the Romanists make of it. Therefore Luther hammers away at the same arguments in practically the same words to both Alveld and Ambrosius Catharinus. To Alveld he says, "Where Baptism and the Gospel are, no one may doubt that there are saints, even if it be only babes in their cradles. But neither Rome nor the papal power is a mark of the Church, for that power cannot make Christians, as Baptism and the Gospel do; and therefore it does not belong to the true Church and is but a human ordinance."³ This, then, is the criterion for a true mark of the Church: it is life-giving; it "makes Christians." Yes, "the Church owes its life to the Word of Christ through faith, and is nourished and preserved by this same Word, that is to say, the promises of God make the Church, not the Church the promise of God."⁴

Luther does not answer outright the question whether Word and Sacraments belong to the nature of the Church. Since, however, he makes it clear that the Church cannot exist without them, it can hardly be misleading to say that they are of the essence of the Church. At least it is hardly going too far to say with Sohm, "The essence of the 'congregatio sanctorum' (the Church of Christ) consists in this, that it is the communion of the right administration of Word and Sacraments, that in it and through it (through its agency) Christ, God, lives on earth with His Word."⁵

---
²*Ibid.*, 721, L. 3.
³*Von dem Papstthum zu Rom.* W. VI, 301, L. 3. Holman, I. 361.
⁴*De captivitate Babylonica*, 1520. W. VI, 560, L. 33. Holman, II. 273.
⁵Rudolph Sohm, *Weltliches und geistliches Recht*, p. 45. München und Leipzig: Duncker und Humblot, 1914.

THE WORD

Against the "visible" sacramental Roman Church, Luther emphasizes the preeminence of the Word. Where the Word is not found (as we see in the Synagogue of Papists and Thomists), there we can be sure "that the Church is not," even though they baptize and partake from the altar. But there we may know Babylon is present. For the Gospel is above bread and Baptism, the "most certain and noble symbol of the Church, since through the Gospel alone it is conceived, formed, kept alive, born, brought up, nourished, clothed, adorned, made strong, armed, preserved, in short, the whole *life* and substance of the Church is in the Word of God, as Christ says 'in every word that proceedeth out of the mouth of God.' "[6]

What is this Word, which is a mark of the Church? That question is important because there are scholars like Troeltsch who intimate that in Luther it is simply the written Word, or the Bible.[7] But Luther emphasizes repeatedly that it is not merely the written Word but the spoken Word. "I speak," he says, "not concerning the written but the spoken Gospel. Not concerning any old harangue, which is declaimed from a platform in temples, but concerning the unadulterated and genuine Word, which teaches the true faith of Christ, not with deformed Thomist faith, which has become silent throughout the whole world, extinguished and suffocated by the Pope and Papists."[8] Christ demanded nothing from his apostles with so much importunity as that they should preach the Gospel. He bade Peter, in the person

---
[6] *Ad . . . Ambrosii Catharini.* W. VII, 721, L. 4.
[7] *The Social Teaching of the Christian Churches,* Vol. II, p. 470. New York: Macmillan, 1931.
[8] *Ad . . . Ambrosii Catharini.* W. VII, 721, L. 15.

of all pastors, feed his sheep, that is, teach the Gospel "viva voce." Therefore he who teaches the Gospel, he is pope, he is the successor of Peter. He who does not is a Judas, a traitor to Christ. For it is only by the publicly preached Gospel that it may be known where the Church and the mystery of the Kingdom of Heaven are.[9] Walther has come to the same conclusion when he says, "Thus he has given also here the answer to the question, how one can get to know the Church to which one must cling: not by the character of the persons, for 'who can know who truly believes or not'[10] but by the preaching of the Word of God."[11]

Thus, with all the emphasis he places on these marks of the Church, Luther never for a moment means that they are to make the Church visible. They only make it perceptible to faith so that the believer may know where to find his own. For even as the protruding ends of the staves led God's people to believe that the ark was present in the holy of holies (I Kings 8:8), so "no one sees the Church, but only believes through the sign of the Word which can only resound in the Church through the Holy Spirit." Therefore the Church in Psalm 9 is called *Almuth*, hidden, and an article of faith confessing that we believe in the Holy Catholic Church confesses that the same is nowhere and never visible. It separates it from every place and person, as Paul says, "In Christ Jesus is neither male nor female, barbarian nor Greek, . . . but ye are all one in Christ Jesus."[12]

The Word, always the Word, says Luther, is the sure sign by which we may know that the Church is present

---
[9]*Ibid.*, 722, L. 3.
[10]*Von dem Papstthum zu Rom.* Erlangen XXVII, 103.
[11]Walther. *Op. cit.*, v. 4, p. 27.
[12]*Ad . . . Ambrosii Catharini.* W. VII, 722, L. 4.

and that Christ is there ruling His Church. In his exposition of the 110th Psalm, Luther says that the "scepter," or "rod," in verse 2 "is the office of preaching (Predigtamt), which the Lord Christ Himself began, and then commanded His messengers, the apostles and their successors, to carry further."[13] This is the only scepter by which He is going to rule His Church, and it is the only mark by which His Kingdom may be known. This preaching office, or Predigtamt, as he calls it, is not a priest's cult or class. It is simply the oral preaching of the Gospel. For Luther goes on to say that Christ shall govern and propagate His Kingdom through no other means than "alone through the oral Word or preaching" ("allein durch das mündliche Wort oder Predigtamt").

When Luther speaks in that way about the Word and preaching, he means ordinarily the Word which has its center in the Gospel of Christ, the Word made flesh. He thus says a little later in the same work that the Church is not going to be ruled by force or law, but by the Word or preaching "which proclaims how we can be saved, i.e., redeemed from sins or death, and brought to everlasting righteousness and life through this Lord and King."[14] This is not only Christ's way of ruling His Church. It is the sure sign that Christ is present, living and working His miracles of grace. For, says Luther, "where the Gospel is, there is Christ. Where Christ is, there is the Holy Ghost and His Kingdom."[15] When therefore Luther from time to time uses the old Augustinian phrase, *"Extra ecclesia nulla salus,"* it must be

---
[13]*Der 110 Psalm, Dixit Dominus, gepredigt und ausgelegt.* 1539. Erlangen XL, 87.
[14]*Ibid.,* 90.
[15]*Predigten am zwanzigsten Sonntage nach Trinitatis, I. 1533.* Erlangen V, 178.

understood in the light of this fact. "God has determined that no one shall or can believe, or receive the Holy Ghost, without the Gospel being orally preached or taught."[16] Therefore, "whoever wants to find Christ must first find the Church. . . . For outside of the Christian Church there is no truth, no Christ, no salvation."[17]

While it is Luther's doctrine of the Communion of Saints which needs to be revived in the consciousness of the believers, it is on the line of the centrality of the Word that the real battle lies. That means the battle against error in the Church on the one hand and the battle against unbelief on the other. This was the line on which the battle of the Reformation was fought and won.

It is impossible to understand Luther and his spiritualized conception of the Church unless we understand his distinction between the written Word and the preached Word. The written Word may be present anywhere. But a lodge is not, nor does it contain, the Church simply because the Bible lies open on the desk and is perhaps even read aloud. The Word there is not a mark of the Church. Luther says: "The most emphatic visible sign of the Church is the Gospel: and I speak not concerning the written, but the spoken Gospel."[18] "God has decreed that no one shall or can believe or receive the Holy Ghost unless the Gospel is preached by word of mouth."[19] It is the spoken Word which is the life-giving power in the Church and therefore is a true mark of the Church. When the Word of God goes forth from a believing mouth, then it is a living Word, which can save

---

[16] *Auslegung des ersten und zweiten Kapitels Johannis*, 1537 und 1538, hier Kap. 1, 1-18. Erlangen, XLV, 87.
[17] *Das Evangelium am II. Christtage.* Erlangen, X, 162.
[18] *Ad . . . Ambrosii Catharini.* Op. var. arg., V, 311.
[19] *Auslegung des ersten und zweiten Kapitels Johannis.* Erlangen, XLV, 358.

men from death, forgive their sins, and lift them into heaven."[20]

In all his preaching Luther never allows a doctrine to become a dead theory to be buried in a volume of dogmatics. His preaching is alive and meant to live by, because the doctrine he preaches is alive, it is "the power of God." So this doctrine of the Word in the Church he brings as a great and abiding comfort to all believers. For there are times when Christians look for the Church and are confused. What they are wont to call the Church appears to be just another society or organization. And there they see a motley crowd of good and bad people, corruption, intrigue, politics, greed, falsehood, and oppression. What has the Church to do in all this? Is the Church still there, or has it been swallowed up in human frailty?

Luther gives a comforting answer to the fearful Christian. He says the devil may succeed in casting a veil of corruption and offense over the Church. Even God may permit it to be hidden behind a cloud of error and sin. But be of good cheer, "as long as the Word of the Gospel remains pure with us and we love and honor it, we need not doubt that Christ is with us, even when things are at their worst."[21] We must still confess, "I believe in the Holy Christian Church." For this is an article of faith and not something we can see.

THE PERENNIAL REFORMATION

We are living in the age of the Reformation! The glory of Rome—or the shadow of Rome—whichever way one

---

[20] *Auslegung des 6. 7. und 8. Kapitels des Evangeliums Johannis*, 1530-15. Erlangen, XLVIII, 207.
[21] *Vorrede auf die Offenbarung S. Johannis.* Erlangen, LXIII, 168.

chooses to look at it, is encompassing the earth. Every Christian rejoices to see the Church marching on. But he wants to be sure that it is the Church. Every Protestant Christian should, basically and historically, have the same idea of the Church as Luther had, that the Church is the fellowship of believers, and that it is present wherever the Word is preached and the Sacraments are rightly administered. We have the same passionate longing for unity in the Church that Luther had. But we believe, as he did, in the centrality of the Word, of faith, and of grace. Sola Scriptura, sola gratia, sola fides is more than a slogan. It means that the Word alone is our final authority in matters of faith and life—not the Word plus tradition. It means that we are saved by the grace of God through faith in the crucified and risen Christ—not through faith plus works.

While we desire outward unity in the Church, including fellowship with Rome, we are still compelled to stand on the ground of the Reformation. We still refuse to place tradition beside Scripture as our final authority for truth. We still are unable to permit good works to be put beside faith as the way of justification before God. We still abhor as unscriptural all the derivatives of this false position; illegitimate children of this incestuous marriage: penances, purgatory, indulgences, satisfactions, supererrogation of merits, prayers to the Virgin and the saints, the sacrifice of the Mass, and the whole system of merits. Like Melanchthon in our Confessions, we could put up with a pope. But we will regard as anti-Christ any man who sets himself up as the vicar of Christ on earth and claims to speak infallibly ex cathedra. We regard the Roman Church as the agent of Satan in her practice of persecuting Christians who will not submit to her dominion, a practice which is as universal today as it has been for a thousand years and more.

In this situation Protestants must still continue to live in the age of the Reformation or, more accurately, to bring the Reformation into the present. In other words, the struggle which was the Reformation must go on. The fight for truth must go on. The Word of grace must still be preached in a thousand dark corners of the world where souls are rotting in tyranny to Law under the cold shadow of the Mass because they have never heard the Gospel of free grace in Christ Jesus.

To call Rome to reform, to clean house on all her unscriptural teachings and practices will hardly produce the batting of an eye in the great Roman Church. She is so much bigger and stronger that she can laugh at us as Goliath laughed at David, and continue to roll on with relentless power. And today she is rolling with all her power. Can anything stop her? Should she be stopped? In so far as she is promoting the truth, no. In so far as she is spreading error and persecuting the truth, yes! And every intelligent non-Roman Christian knows that she is persecuting the truth and trying to demolish all non-Roman Christianity. For those reasons and for the cause of the Kingdom of Christ non-Roman Christendom has begun to pray militantly to God either to reform Rome or to stop her!

The Lutheran Church believes there is only one way to do this job, as far as men are called upon to do it. The way is not to try to meet Rome on her own ground.

In the first place, it is not by the way of playing a smarter game of politics. The Roman hierarchy is the strongest political machine in existence. It can present a united front on any issue, because it has one head and one leadership and can speak with one voice. Even if we would, we could not put a lobby in Washington that could compete for one moment with the National Catholic Welfare Conference in our national capital. Even if we know that it is "the intention of that church to establish itself as the state church in this country,"[22] we cannot hope to challenge her on that line. Neither do we care to. Our Lord said, "My kingdom is not of this world," and nothing is clearer than His complete rejection of promoting the Kingdom through political power. The President's personal ambassador to the Vatican and Spellman's spectacular pilgrimage are good headline stuff and a grand show of political power. But Christ still says, "My kingdom is not of this world." Let us leave this field of politics to Rome.

In the second place, we can rule out the way of church finance. All the wealth of the non-Roman churches would make a sorry sight compared to the fabulous wealth of the Holy See. Furthermore, the way many Protestant churches are using their money will not seriously affect the forward march of Rome.

Likewise, we ought to begin to think twice when we shout that the answer lies in a united Protestantism. A glorious vision, yes, and a great hope. But united about what? United for what? United around a scientific program of social betterment? United around the brotherhood of man and the fatherhood of God? United around the least common denominator of Scriptural doctrine? United to bring about economic equality?

Rome smiles at the slogans and programs and move-

---

[22]Harold E. Fey, *Can Catholicism Win America?* (A series of eight articles reprinted from *The Christian Century*, contained in the issues of Nov. 29, 1944, to Jan. 17, 1945), p. 21. Chicago: 1945.

ments of Protestantism. How well she knows that all these things are quack remedies for a sick church, emergency measures, shots in the dark of a church that has lost its direction.

Protestantism, even the Lutheran Church, has been naive along these lines. But one thing it cannot forget, though it may have temporarily forgotten it. The only thing that has ever been able to stop the Roman Church or reform it or cleanse it has been the preaching and the free dissemination of the Word of God. The Lutheran Reformation accomplished it to a degree that has never been equalled before or since. And Luther had only one weapon, the Word of God, preached in the churches, proclaimed from the house tops, taught in the homes and in every conceivable circle, public and private, and poured out in a flood of literature to all people of all classes.

What happened? The Reformation! Millions of Roman Catholics forsook their Church to breathe again the free air of evangelical Christianity, so that Pope Pius IV, "in a moment of discouragement, perhaps, told the cardinals that scarcely a tenth part of Christendom obeyed him."[23] And this was only 19 years after the death of Luther. But there came also a reformation within the Roman Church, which had gained such momentum that it continued long after Luther had been excommunicated and driven out of the Roman communion.

Lay the credit for the counter-reformation to the Jesuits and the Inquisition or to the Council of Trent, or both, if you please. The fact remains that the counter-reformation was a spiritual movement which "brought forth new religious forces, and opened up, even for

---

[23]Turner, Edward Raymond, *Europe 1450-1789*, p. 190. New York: Doubleday, Page & Co., 1923.

them, a new path of development."[24] And the thing that brought about that "spiritual reform" was the incalculable power of the Word of God which Luther had preached and broadcast through the Church.

And here lies the great tragedy, the greatest, perhaps, in the history of the Church. A Roman priest told a friend of mine in Minneapolis a few years ago, "When I am together with you and your fine Christian family, I become sadly aware of how much the Roman Catholic Church lost when it lost Luther."

What if Luther had been allowed to stay in the Roman Church and continue to preach the Word? Only God knows. But there is no reason to doubt that the cleansing process which he started would have gone on, that errors would have been corrected, abuses abolished, and that the preaching of the Gospel would have kindled a purging fire that might have spread through the length and breadth of the Christian Church.

But everything that did happen happened by the power of the Gospel that was let loose by the Reformers. Now what has that to do with us in the middle of the twentieth century? Does it not mean an awakening to the fact that there is still only one way to meet the "problem of Rome," and that is by proclaiming the Word of God, by broadcasting to the ends of the earth the Gospel of God's love in Christ Jesus our crucified and risen Savior? "For God so loved the world, that he gave his only begotten Son, that whosoever believeth in him should not perish, but have everlasting life" (John 3:16). This is the heart of the Bible, which is the Word of God, His revelation of His will for the salvation of men.

---

[24]Rudolph Sohm, *Outlines of Church History*, p. 180. London: Macmillan & Co., 1921.

The Lutheran Church believes and confesses that the Bible is the Word of God, that it is the truth of God for all time. If the world or any part of it is to be saved and sanctified, it must be accomplished through the Word of God. For the Gospel of Christ is "the power of God unto salvation to every one that believeth" (Rom. 1:16). And Christ prayed to the Father, "Sanctify them through thy truth: thy word is truth" (John 17:17). So whether we think of the conversion of the unbeliever, the purging of Rome, or the coming alive again of Protestantism, there is only one way to bring it to pass, that is the proclamation of the Word of God. That means to fill the air with the Gospel of Christ, spoken, written, broadcast, photographed, projected on the screen. Let the churches again echo with the Word of God and drive out all the humanistic prattle that is cursing Protestantism. Let the errors of the Mass be subjected to the regular preaching of the Word and they will begin to drop off like dead leaves in the wind. Let every pastor, minister, preacher and priest make it his paramount business to preach the Word in season and out of season. Let every home build its life around the Word of God. Let every Christian search the Scriptures daily and live on them and by them as the Bread of Life. "If ye continue in my word, then are ye my disciples indeed; and ye shall know the truth, and the truth shall make you free" (John 8:31, 32).

If this is our strategy for the Kingdom, then the Word must become the most precious possession in life for all of us. And this means the Word which has Christ at the center, crucified and risen, living and reigning in His Church. It means something beyond boasting that we have the truth. Too many of us have gone to sleep on that pillow. Luther sounds the warning to his followers:

"When we have God's Word pure and clear, then we think ourselves all right; we become negligent, and repose in a vain security; we no longer pay due heed, thinking it will always so remain; we do not watch and pray against the devil, who is ready to tear the divine Word out of our hearts. It is with us as with travelers, who, so long as they are on the highway, are tranquil and heedless, but if they go astray into woods or cross paths, uneasily seek which way to take, this or that."[25]

How mysteriously God works to preserve His Church and to disarm her enemies. When we consider the numbers and the might of the enemies of Christ, is it not astounding that they have left us the one weapon with which we can overpower them? Astounding, yes. But let us remember that it is not due to the stupidity of our enemies but to the mercy of God. It is His way of carrying out His promise, "The gates of hell shall not prevail against my church." He has put in our hands an invincible weapon, "the sword of the Spirit, which is the word of God." Let us wake up and wield it! Men must listen or die. It is 400 years since Luther sounded the alarm. It fits our day. He said, "The great unthankfulness, contempt of God's Word, and wilfulness of the world, make me fear that the divine light will soon cease to shine on man, for God's Word has ever had its certain course. . . . Greece and many other countries have heard the Word of God, but have abandoned it, and it is to be feared even now it may quit Germany, and go into other lands. I hope the last day will not be long delayed. The darkness grows thicker around us, and godly servants of the Most High become rarer and more rare. Impiety and licen-

---

[25] *The Table Talk of Martin Luther.* Tr. by William Hazlitt, p. 8. Philadelphia: United Lutheran Publication House.

tiousness are rampant throughout the world, and we live like pigs, like wild beasts, devoid of all reason. But a voice will soon be heard thundering forth: Behold the Bridegroom cometh. God will not be able to bear this wicked world much longer, but will come with the dreadful day, and chastise the scorners of His Word."[26]

---

[26] *Ibid.*, p. 8f.

CHAPTER NINE

THE *Experience* OF HOLY COMMUNION

"I believe in the Holy Ghost, the Holy Christian Church, the Communion of Saints." "I believe in one holy catholic and Apostolic Church." When God's people throughout the world make that solemn confession they are acknowledging that the Church is an object of faith. It is a spiritual and invisible communion. Hence it is perceptible only to faith. For I cannot touch it. I cannot see it. I cannot count the members of it. I can see the buildings. I can see people going in to worship. I can see the marks of it in Word and Sacrament. But the Church in which I believe I cannot see. With Luther, "I believe that there is on earth through the whole wide world no more than one holy, common, Christian Church, which is nothing else than the congregation, or assembly of the saints, *i.e.*, the pious, believing men on earth, which is gathered, preserved, and ruled by the Holy Ghost, and daily increased by means of the Sacraments and the Word of God."

But this faith in the Communion of Saints is no more a purely intellectual faith than faith in Christ Himself. I believe that Christ is what He claims to be. But much more, I trust in Him as my Savior from sin, I embrace Him in an active conscious faith whereby I "experience Christ" with all the spiritual blessings that He holds in Himself for me. In the same way I believe that the Church is what Scripture says it is, the Communion of Saints and the Body of Christ, the very Kingdom of God. But more, I embrace the Church, the Communion of Saints, as my holy Mother, and in a conscious act of faith I make my own all the spiritual blessings that the Church represents.

To illustrate, think of a little desert flower. It may stand there in the blistering heat and bleak barrenness of the desert, or it may be transplanted and stand in the loveliest garden. But the flower blooms as sweetly in one place as in the other. Apparently it makes no difference to the flower where it is.

Not so with man. He may stand in the world unregenerate and up to his neck in sin and guilt. Or he may stand in the Kingdom of God in this same world, cleansed by the blood of the Lamb. Would anyone suppose that his mental attitudes and emotional experiences would be the same in one place as in the other? Certainly not. He is a new creature. He has been clothed with the righteousness of Christ. He has experienced the joy of forgiveness. He has experienced Christ. And this is no single momentary experience that once entered the man's life and then flitted away to return no more or, at best, on rare occasions. It is a continuous experience, this experience of Christ, though indeed it fluctuates like a barometer in intensity. It is something we live on, live by, something we enjoy. The awareness of communion with Christ is a living experience which fills us with joy and strength. For we must not forget that this communion represents a state of grace. Hence in it we are bound around and upheld by the grace of God which is in Christ Jesus.

Of the same nature and a vital part of this communion with Christ is the experience of the Communion of Saints. At the risk of being misunderstood, we might also reverse that and say that the experience of Christ is the vital part of the experience of the Communion of Saints. For as Luther says, "In this Christian Church *He* daily and richly forgives me and all believers all our sins." In other words, to experience the Communion of Saints is to experience Christ Himself. But it is more than that, more than a personal and individual experience of Christ. It is the experience of Christ in and through all the saints. It is an awareness that because I am one with Christ I am one with all the saints. For together we are the Body of Christ, and we are "members one of another."

The weakness of sectarian Christianity lies at this point. The primary emphasis is right: personal communion with Christ. But these brethren throw overboard the whole treasury of spiritual values which our Lord has given us in the fact of the Communion of Saints. The sectarian is a lonely man. He is like the desert flower. He is content to bask in the sunshine of God. Whether he basks alone in the desert of his self-sufficiency or in the company of a host of equally radiant flowers seems to make no difference to him. In fact he prefers the lonely desert to the garden. It appears not to enter his mind that some of the flowers in the garden may even be more radiant than he is. Does he forget that their radiance might increase his own? Does he overlook the possibility of sharing some of his own radiance with the less radiant ones? Or does he perchance prefer to be a lone star which appears to shine more brightly because there are no other stars around? One is tempted to ask, without being facetious, "Has the good Lord arranged for soloists in the heavenly choir?"

A Christian who has not yet attained to an experience of the fact of the Communion of Saints is still living in spiritual poverty. And the day he makes the *great* discovery will be a day of rejoicing in his life. Surely one of the most glorious experiences in all eternity will be when we stand in the midst of the great white host who "have washed their robes, and made them white in the blood of the Lamb." And in the midst, by the grace of God, stand I! "Blessing, and honor, and glory, and power, be unto him that sitteth upon the throne, and unto the Lamb for ever and ever."

But must I wait till that day for the great discovery? On the contrary, God has graciously ordained that even in this vale of tears I may join that happy pilgrim band and blend my voice with the choir of the redeemed in praise to the Lamb. "Glorious things are spoken of Thee, O city of God" (Ps. 87).

The unhappy fact of Protestant Christianity has been the spectacle of individual Christians straggling along the pilgrim road, each singing, or trying to sing, the same song, but each in his own way, oblivious of the choir that marches on ahead, yes, sometimes even competing with it.

It is the picture of the Church which Screwtape gives his Satanic Majesty, as he writes to Wormwood in hell, reporting on the progress of his battle with the forces of Light in the world:

"The Church herself is, of course, heavenly defended and we have not yet quite succeeded in giving her *all* the characteristics of a faction; but subordinate factions within her have often produced admirable results, from the parties of Paul and Apollos at Corinth down to the High and Low parties in the Church of England."[1]

This Protestant individualism, this lone-wolf Christianity, is a foreign growth. Sometimes it appears in a whole group, and we call it a sect. Why? Because a sect, says Webster, is "a part cut off." It stands alone. It may be a Christian group. But it is totally indifferent to the whole Christian Church. It forgets that the Church is *one*. It flaunts its self-sufficiency in the face of the Body of Christ like a lewd woman putting on airs before the figure of the blessed Virgin. Do such groups hold their tongue in their cheek when they confess: "I believe in the holy Christian Church, the Communion of Saints"? Doesn't the whole attitude smack of the factiousness which St. Paul condemns among the Corinthians?

Sometimes the phenomenon appears in the shape of an individual, and we call him a lone-wolf Christian. He takes his Christianity in secret, and he keeps it securely hidden in his inside pocket. He doesn't belong to the organized Church. It has too many hypocrites. "Me and God," that's all that matters. If you ask him about his faith, he may say, It's none of your business. What ails the man? Is it the old superiority complex of the Pharisee, saying to God, "I thank Thee, that I am not as other men are"? Or is it the man who wants to have one foot in heaven and one in the world? Being ashamed of it, he would rather not discuss it. He might give himself away.

O unhappy sect! O lonely pilgrim! God has planted you in a garden, and you run your tendrils out into the road to be trampled on, or into the weeds to be choked, or into the woods to be lost in the big black forest. If Christ has made you rich, how can you keep Him to

---
[1] C. S. Lewis, *Screwtape Letters*, p. 41. New York: Macmillan, 1943.

yourself while your neighbor is dying in spiritual poverty? If you have had a taste of the power of Christ in your life, why do you cut yourself off from the power house, which is the Church? Who wants to be alone in heaven? Nobody. "An eternal happiness, an immeasurable heaven of joy, and only one to enjoy it, only one, even if that one be I myself! No! Alone, I could not be happy."[2]

But the forecourts of heaven are opened to us here on earth in the Church of Jesus Christ. "Behold the Church! It is the contrary of loneliness—blessed fellowship! Millions of the blessed and of believers—who are becoming blessed—and, in the midst of their songs of praise, the Lord!—No longer lonely, but permeated, satisfied—yes, blessed is he who is one of the millions, each of whom has Christ, and with Him heaven and earth!"[3]

In the Communion of Saints there lies a great new world waiting to be discovered by millions of Christians. How can we enter into that world and into that great experience? In no other way than we experience every other blessing of God.

IT IS GOD WHO BRINGS US INTO THE CHURCH THROUGH THE MEANS OF GRACE

"Acceptance into this great spiritual body, with its variety of manifestations, is not something which we can achieve for ourselves. We cannot enter it by frantic efforts to find companionship or by forming organizations, in order to escape solitude. The fellowship which the early Christians knew as *koinonia* was much rather something which they had not themselves created, but which they

---

[2]William Loehe, *Three Books Concerning the Church*. Translated by E. T. Horn, p. 4. Reading, Pa.: Pilger Publishing House, 1908.
[3]Ibid., p. 8.

had received as the gift of God. On the day of our conversion we rejoice in the knowledge that from now on we are delivered from all isolation, and are caught up in a current which flows around the whole world."[4]

God plants us in His Church in holy Baptism. Christ binds us to Himself through His Word. But this Communion with Christ and with all believers is experienced and is testified to most strongly of all in the partaking of the Lord's Supper. For there is not only the *koinonia* as described in the New Testament, but there is also a peculiar separation of those who love the Lord, banded together and giving testimony to their faith and their membership in the Body of Christ. Luther in his Sermon on the Blessed Sacrament delivered on Maundy Thursday, 1534, on I Cor. 11:23-26, brings out the uniqueness of the Communion in the Supper. He says it is not only necessary to come together to hear preaching of the Word, but we must also come together "at one Table, and eat and drink with one another."[5] When we hear the Word it is quite possible that there is one present who is an enemy of the Lord. Hence though the Gospel also holds the Christians together . . . yet this Supper does it much more (although hypocrites may be present), for every Christian confesses publicly and for himself what he believes. There those who do not belong are separated. And those who are of one faith, with one hope and heart toward the Lord, find themselves together. Hence it is called in Latin "communio." And through this Communion our Lord holds His little flock together.

To bring out this fact of Communion, Luther uses a

---
[4] Karl Heim, *The Church of Christ and the Problems of the Day*, pp. 118-119. New York: Scribner's, 1935.
[5] Erlangen, II, 209.

striking illustration. Bread and wine were the elements our Lord chose to convey His grace. Every kernel of corn has its own life and form. Yet when all the kernels are ground together they form one bread. So every man is a particular person and creature. Yet when in the Sacrament we partake of the one bread we all become one bread, one body (I Cor. 10). Likewise the individual grapes are pressed together to make the one beautiful wine. So Christians in the Sacrament. And the Lord uses the Sacrament to make us all one in mind, doctrine, and faith. Position, power, sex, office, make no difference. For in Christ is neither man nor wife, prince nor peasant, but only believers in Christ.

This sense of Communion bridges all distances, says Luther in the same sermon. I am here. Another is in Jerusalem. We are total strangers to one another. Yet by faith we are one Body, and Christ the Head.

The *purpose* of the Sacrament, too, says Luther, is expressed in this term Communion. While Luther in his later works emphasizes above all forgiveness of sins as the principal purpose and blessing in the Sacrament, his earlier works stress the communion with Christ and the saints.[6] It may be that when the Reformation schism had been accomplished and the outward unity broken, Luther realized more keenly the inner unity of the Church. Certain it is from those works that to him the sense of the Communion of Saints was a real and deep experience. And the deepest moment of that experience he found in the Lord's Supper. To a generation like ours, where indifference to the Lord's Supper has become a habit and —we must confess it with shame—even a characteristic of

---

[6]Hans Stöcker. "Grundzüge aus Luthers Abendmahlslehre in ihrer entwicklung 1519-1529." *Luthertum*, hft. 5, pp. 129-142, 1938.

the Protestant Church, Luther has something arresting to say. The Protestant Church today as a whole has no passion for the blessed Sacrament. She has no appreciation of the Communion of Saints in the Body of Christ. She is spiritually bankrupt. Isn't there some connection? Is Sasse right in his analysis of our spiritual stagnation, when he says, "Where the habit of church-going has disappeared and the congregation is left dead or dying, there is only one means of bringing the people back to church. There must be awakened in them a hunger and a thirst for the Lord's Supper. Where that hunger and that thirst is awakened—and certainly it is not in our power to awaken it—people will go back to church. For the hunger and thirst for the Word of God can be satisfied at home (im Kämmerlein)—at least according to the Pietistic theory by which the Protestantism of both the last two centuries has preached her churches empty. The Sacrament of the Altar, on the contrary, except where one is seriously ill, is only received in the House of God."[7]

If the ecumenical movement is achieving anything, it is the revival in Protestantism of the concept of the Church as the holy Christian Church, the Communion of Saints. It is a portent of future growth in this realm of the Christian life that the Edinburgh Conference on Faith and Order could make the unanimous declaration, "We use the term 'communion of saints' as meaning that all who are 'in Christ' are knit together in one fellowship through the Holy Spirit. This conception, which is found repeatedly in the Scriptures, occurs as a phrase of the Apostles' Creed, and gives expression to a precious truth for all Christians."

---

[7]H. Sasse. *Kirche und Herrenmahl* (Bekennende Kirche. hft. 59-60), p. 34. Munich: Chr. Kaiser Verlag, 1938.

But a tragic shadow hangs over this encouraging note. How can this sense of the Communion of Saints reach any degree of depth in Protestantism until we can share together the deepest "communion experience" of all in the holy communion of the Lord's Supper? And what hope is there for that experience when the Real Presence of the Lord's Body and Blood is a fact to some and a myth to others? Is it a vain hope to pray that the contemporary swing of Protestant theology back to a transcendent God and an authoritative Scripture might eventually carry with it a return to faith in the Real Presence? Without such a "return" there is hardly any purpose in pleading for a revival of interest in the Lord's Supper in Protestantism. For without the Real Presence the Sacrament must of necessity remain a "secondary" matter in the life of the Church.

The corollary to this is that in that segment of Protestantism where the Real Presence is recognized, there must be a restoration of the Sacrament to a central place in the Church's worship life. This is imperative not only on the basis of history and the practice of the Early Church. It is of the very nature of the case.

Protestantism's indifference to the Lord's Supper and obliviousness to the Communion of Saints is a besetting sin from two angles; and it is the ministry that must bear the brunt of the guilt, for not making the Sacrament available. Spiritually speaking it is both suicide and murder. It is a pauperizing neglect of God's gift of grace on the one hand and a selfish neglect of duty on the other. For the experience of the Communion of Saints in the Sacrament has a twofold aspect. It is both privilege and obligation.

In his Gospel preaching Luther was urgent in his appeal to his people to attend the Sacrament faithfully that they might experience the blessings of the Communion of Saints. This was not any perfunctory preaching of a nice theory. It was a burning Gospel message breathing his own experience. He was preaching to sinners in anguish of soul when he called the weak in faith to cling to the external signs and feel himself transported into perfect communion with Christ and His Body, the Church. His burdens become their burdens. And if his sins terrify him, he shall let himself be carried to the Lord's Table in the arms of Mother Church, as the paralytic on his bed, and the Lord will receive him on the faith of his fellow-believers.[8]

The sense of spiritual solidarity, of oneness with the saints, of communion with the strong, is something you should expect all Christians to be looking for. But apparently they are not. Or else they do not know that such a thing exists. Or possibly they want it, yet do not know where to find it. Why should we be weak when we can be strong? Why should we walk in solitary loneliness, when we could be swinging along the King's highway with a band of singing saints? An only child is an unfortunate child, and often unhappy. So is a "lone wolf" Christian. And to break into the family is not only to join a church. That is a necessary part, but only a part, the external part. To really break in and become one with the family of God is for the Christian to go to the Lord's Supper. There he really enters into the family of kindred spirits. He begins to "experience" the *community* of Christians, a community whose roots reach down into the very wounds of Christ. And with the Blood of

---

[8]*Sermo de digna preparatione cordis* . . . 1518. W. I, 333. L. 13ff., L. 25.

Christ coursing through their veins, they are drawn closer than brothers. For they are the Body of Christ!

This community or communion lies at the very heart of the Sacrament. Luther says in his "Sermon on the Brotherhoods and the Sacrament," "The significance or purpose of this sacrament[9] is the fellowship of saints, whence it derives its common name *synaxis* or *communio,* that is, fellowship; and *communicare* means to take part in this fellowship, or, as we say, to go to the sacrament, because Christ and all saints are one spiritual body, just as the inhabitants of a city are one community and body, each citizen being a member of the other and a member of the entire city. All the saints, therefore, are members of Christ and of the Church, which is a spiritual and eternal city of God, and whoever is taken into this city is said to be received into the communion of saints, and to be incorporated into Christ's spiritual body and made a member of Him. . . . To receive the bread and wine of this Sacrament, then, is nothing else than to receive a sure sign of this fellowship and incorporation with Christ and all saints."[10]

Luther never allows us to forget the great fact that the Church is the Communion of Saints. But it is also a communion of *sinners* in the Body of Christ. It is "for sinners only." It is only as a sinner, conscious of the damning power of sin, that I will flee to the Cross to be embraced by the bleeding Savior. It is only as a sinner that I throw my wretched self into the arms of Mother Church. For the key to my release is forgiveness. And there again it is in the blessed Sacrament that the key of forgiveness opens the door wide into the Communion of Saints. And

---
[9] W. II, 743. Holman, II. 10.
[10] *Ibid.,* W. II, 743, L. 7-22, H. II, 10.

there Luther revels in the blessings that surround him. "The fellowship is of such a nature that all the spiritual possessions of Christ and His saints are imparted and communicated to him who receives this sacrament; and further, all his sufferings and sins are communicated to them, and thus love engenders love and unites all."[11]

This is no peripheral matter, no plaything, that Luther is toying with. He is at the very heart of the Christian life, where there is a life and death struggle with sin going on. "O wretched man that I am! who shall deliver me from the body of this death?" There is no answer but the one St. Paul gives: "I thank God through Jesus Christ our Lord." And in the blessed Sacrament I find Him reaching out those wounded hands to enfold me and to heal my wounds of sin. Luther cries out with the pleading urgency of an Isaiah calling sinners to come to the waters. It is for just such a struggling, lonely sinner Christ and all the saints are waiting in the Sacrament. "It is given only to those who need strength and comfort, who have timid hearts and terrified consciences, and who are assailed by sin, or have even fallen into sin. What could it do for untroubled and falsely secure spirits, which neither need nor desire it? For the Mother of God says, 'He filleth only the hungry, and comforteth them that are distressed.' "[12] To such a one the "immeasurable grace and mercy of God are given in this sacrament." For "if anyone be in despair, if he be distressed by his sinful conscience or terrified by death, or have any other burden on his heart, and desire to be rid of them all, let him go joyfully to the sacrament of the altar and lay down his grief in the midst of the con-

---
[11] *Loc. cit.*
[12] *Ibid.*, 746, L. 16ff. Holman, II. 15.

gregation and seek help from the entire company of the spiritual body." No trouble is too great, no burden too heavy to ask the communion of believers to share with you. "Though I am a sinner and have fallen, though this or that misfortune has befallen me, I will go to the sacrament to receive a sign from God that I have on my side Christ's righteousness, life and sufferings, with all holy angels and all the blessed in heaven, and all pious men on earth."

But the Communion of Saints is not only a treasure house of good things, which I am privileged to draw on daily. It is also a thing to which I can contribute by sharing what God has given me and by putting my shoulder under the burdens my brothers are carrying. We can call this an obligation if we wish. But to the friend of Christ it is on a higher level than duty. It is a grateful exercise of the law of love. If the love of Christ moves me, with St. Paul, to desire to "know the fellowship of His sufferings," He has opened the door for me in the sufferings of my brother. For we are together members of the Body of Christ, and "if one member suffer, all the members suffer."[13] Do we see our friends outside the Church going to the devil because they do not know Jesus Christ, the Son of God, the Savior of the world? The anguish of our Lord over those unforgiven sinners pressed drops of blood from His brow in Gethsemane and broke His heart on Calvary. But we are the Body of Christ. Does not "the fellowship of His sufferings" impel us in the Church to carry that burden with Him and with all the saints, until the lost be saved?

"There are," says Luther, "those . . . who would share the benefits but not the cost," and who, "because they

---
[13] W. VI, 131, L. 12.

fear the world, are unwilling in their turn to contribute to this fellowship, to help the poor, to endure sins, to care for the sick ... No, we on our part must make the evil of others our own, if we desire Christ and His saints to make our evil their own."[14] We must "be willing to share all the burdens ... of Christ and His saints, their sorrow and their joy."[15] "Then will the fellowship be complete and justice be done to the sacrament."[16]

Do we have to stretch our imagination to see how those words of Luther apply to our generation of war, separation, and world-wide suffering? Certain centuries in the Church's history are reverently called *centuries of suffering and persecution*. The 20th century will no doubt go down in history as one of those centuries. For more Christians have died for their faith under the cruel hand of pagan rulers in the first half of our century than in any century in history. And through that period of suffering the Church has learned, and is learning, that it is in such times she needs the comforting consciousness of the Communion of Saints. It is a fact so universal that the New Testament is full of it. It is the comforting message of the author of Hebrews: "Wherefore seeing that we also are compassed about with so great a cloud of witnesses, let us lay aside every weight, and the sin which doth so easily beset us, and let us run with patience the race that is set before us, looking unto Jesus the author and finisher of our faith" (Heb. 12:1-2). It is the picture of St. Paul writing out of tribulation to the Ephesians, "Wherefore I desire that ye faint not at my tribulations for you, which is your glory. For this cause I bow my

---

[14]*Ein Sermon von Sakrament des Leichnams Christi und von den Brüderschaften.* W. II, 747, L. 26ff. Holman, II. 17.
[15]*Ibid.*, 744. L. 16ff. Holman, II. 12.
[16]*Ibid.*, 748, L. 21. Holman, II. 17.

knees unto the Father of our Lord Jesus Christ, of whom the whole family in heaven and earth is named" (Eph. 3:13-15). The apostle thus extends the concept of the Communion of Saints to the redeemed in heaven, who belong with us to God's "family."

All this is ours in the Church and should be a daily experience of faith. And particularly in the blessed sacrament, where we preëminently partake of the Body of Christ, this experience reaches its most intense reality.

Our so-called "social Gospel Christianity" fades into shallow insignificance beside Luther's conception of the "sin-bearing" and "sin-sharing" which should be the very life of every member of the Church of Christ. Luther seems to understand what it means to be "Christ-like" and to "know the fellowship of his sufferings." The Christian, he says, should be like Christ and should identify himself with the sinner and the sufferer, take his yoke upon himself. Luther condemns monasticism and every false asceticism which, like the Pharisee, see righteousness only within their own walls and with a superior air let the rest of the world be damned. "They don't know that they are to be servants and make their piety serve their neighbor."[17] Instead of being self-sufficient let the Christian throw himself into the situation of his suffering, sin-scarred neighbor. Let him "roll in the sinner's slime so deep that he sticks in it, take his sin upon himself, come out with it and act as if it were his own."[18] "A virgin must don the wreath of a prostitute, a pious wife must put on the veil of an adulteress, and let everything we have be a cloak with which we cover the sinner. All our gifts must be at the service of our neighbor."[19]

---
[17]Predigt am 3. Sonntag nach Trinitatis. W. X, pt. 3, 218.
[18]*Ibid.*, L. 27.
[19]*Ibid.*, 220, 221.

This sin-bearing with one's neighbor also means *intercession*. "This is a good Christian work, when you concern yourself about your neighbor, go into your chamber, and pray: O my God, I hear that my neighbor is suffering under sin, that he is fallen; O Lord, help him up again. Thus you serve your neighbor with true concern."[20]

It is days such as these that bring home to Christians the deep reality and the comfort of this communion of prayer. But to make it a real experience we must bring the whole thing out of the subconscious to the conscious. The dying marine in a foxhole and the sinking sailor on a raft, each can have the blessed comfort that his prayers merge with ours before the throne of grace. He can know that the whole Church of Jesus Christ is carrying him and his suffering body and his aching soul into the arms of our loving Father on the wings of prayer.

Here again it is at the Lord's Supper that this communion of prayer reaches its deepest reality. When one goes to the Sacrament, it is indeed tempting to say, "Surely I have enough with my own sins not to be concerned with others at this moment." But the great Apostle when he spoke of the Sacrament could not tear himself loose from the fact of *koinonia*. "The bread which we break, is it not the communion of the body of Christ? For *we being many are one bread, and one body:* for we are all partakers of that one bread" (I Cor. 10:16-17). Then let me in the Sacrament, in my communion with Christ, reach out for that additional comfort of the oneness and the communion of all who partake with me, whether here or in India or in Guadalcanal. And let me likewise in this hour of holy communion with Christ identify my-

---
[20]*Ibid.*, 219, L. 2.

self with my suffering soldier and my shipwrecked sailor, praying that the gentle Savior will succor them in their pain and grant them forgiveness and peace.

On into the valley of the shadow marches the Church of God with me. Christ is there, the Good Shepherd. And His Church, like a loving Mother, He sends to comfort me and to lead me to the light. With the Word she silences my accusing conscience. With the blessed Sacrament she enfolds me in the embrace of all His saints. With them I am one with Christ. I am a member of His Body. He is the Heart whose redeeming blood streams through the veins of my soul, washing away every stain of my sin. He is the Head who will lead on to eternal glory in His Church triumphant. Now indeed we "are come unto Mount Sion, and unto the city of the living God, the heavenly Jerusalem, and to an innumerable company of angels, to the general assembly and church of the firstborn, which are written in heaven, and to God the judge of all, and to the spirits of just men made perfect, and to Jesus the mediator of the new covenant, and to the blood of sprinkling, that speaketh better things than that of Abel" (Heb. 12:22-24). So with Luther we take hold of this gift of God called the Communion of Saints, as we hear him speak to his dying friend, the Elector, "Is it not good to be here, where if one member suffer, all members suffer with him, if one be honored, all rejoice with him? Thus while I suffer, I no longer suffer alone; Christ and all Christians suffer with me. The faith of the Church succors my agitation, their purity suffers the temptation of my wantonness, their poorness is my gain. . . . Such a thing is the Communion of Saints and the Church of Christ."[21]

---

[21] *Tessaradecas consolatoria pro laborantibus et oneratis.* 1520. W. VI, 131, L. 7ff.

CHAPTER TEN

THE *Keys* OF THE KINGDOM

> "I believe in the holy Christian Church ... the forgiveness of sins."[1]
> "In which Christian Church He forgives daily and richly all sins to me and all believers."[2]

THE NATURE AND PURPOSE OF THE KEYS

If we want to get at Luther's doctrinal position in its simplest form I presume we shall all agree to go to the Small Catechism. Having in his Explanation of the Third Article of the Creed eliminated man's "own reason or strength" as a means of coming to Christ or to faith in Him, he gives all the glory to God who Himself reaches down and "calls, gathers, enlightens, and sanctifies the whole Christian Church on earth, and preserves it in union with Jesus Christ in the one true faith." Thus, says Luther, it is God who creates the Church. He builds it of living stones, and even the stones He must create Himself. He must bring man every step of the way, from the initial "call" to "everlasting life." That is Luther's "grace alone" theology in its simplest form. Yes, we can simplify it still further and ask, "What does God do in

---

[1] The Apostles' Creed.
[2] "The Small Catechism." *Concordia Triglotta*, p. 545. St. Louis: Concordia Publishing House, 1921.

His Church on earth?" Luther's answer is there in one great sentence, "In this Christian Church He daily and richly *forgives* me and all believers all our sins." Forgiveness!

Forgiveness is the thing! Forgiveness is the mind of God planning our redemption before the foundation of the world. Forgiveness is the love of God sending His own Son to die for the sins of men. Forgiveness is the bleeding heart of Christ breaking on Calvary for the sins of the world. Forgiveness is the blood shed on the Cross for our salvation. Forgiveness is the last prayer of the Crucified for sinners, "Father forgive them, for they know not what they do." Forgiveness is the last gift of the dying Savior, whispering in death to a lost sinner, "Today thou shalt be with me in Paradise."

Lowering our sights from God to man, there it is again. Forgiveness is the greatest need of man. Why? Simply because his basic ailment is *sin*. The world seems as close to the brink of chaos as it has ever been. The human mind through scientific investigation has gotten so far that it has finally discovered the secret of natural power by which man can destroy the human race. And there sits man in the lap of Mother Earth, like a scared child sitting in the middle of the school room with a burning firecracker in his hand. What shall he do with it? In a panic of fear and utter helplessness man cries out, My God, what shall I do?

Is God patient enough to hear even such a wild cry in the dark? Why should He? And yet if it is a cry of confession and faith He will. But is it? All Christendom is waiting breathlessly for the voice of bankrupt civilization to say that it is. Where is the voice? From time to time we think we hear it. But alas, the voice is lost in the smashing of atoms and the explosion of bombs and the shout of proud rationalists crying, "See what we have found!" Does God have the patience to listen to man's cry as he sits in panic with the smouldering firecracker in his hand? Who dares to put words in the mouth of the Almighty? And yet I wonder if His answer to materialistic man in this year of our Lord is something like this: "You proud, blundering fool, how long have I warned you against pursuing your own devices without my help and guidance? How long have I pleaded with you to go my way into light and life, instead of your own way into darkness and death? Thousands of years ago I said to your first parents, 'The day thou eatest thereof thou shalt surely die.' They disobeyed and so they died and all must die. I said to Noah's scoffing neighbors, 'Unless you repent of your wickedness and turn to Noah's God you will all be destroyed in the flood which I will send upon the earth.' They continued to scoff at Noah and his God, and they were all destroyed. I said to my own people in the wilderness, 'Follow me, and I will bring you to the promised land.' They rebelled and forsook my chosen leaders, and they were punished with 40 years of painful wandering in the desert. For centuries I warned them, instructed them, pleaded with them. I promised them a Savior and a King. I sent my own Son to earth to become man and to fulfill all my promises of salvation to men. He preached, He taught, He healed the sick, He became the servant of all men. He showed men the one and only way to God and life eternal, the way of faith in Him and love to God and man. And this Jesus, the Son of God, their only hope of salvation, they crucified."

Oh, the patience of God! Instead of giving up all further efforts and letting man go to perdition, the Lord of Glory rises from the dead. He lays the foundation of His Church on earth. He Himself is the Cornerstone. Prophets and apostles, with their God-given testimony and their living faith, furnish the foundation. And one by one He adds the stones, living stones, believers cleansed by His blood; sinners all, but saved by grace. And notice, it is *His* Church. He will build it. To Peter confessing his faith in Him He says, "On this rock I will build my church." It is *His* Church. He will live in it, be the life of it, build it. He will so identify Himself with it that the Church will be called "His Body."

To the Church He gives Himself. What more can He give? Nothing. But He gives Himself in such a way that the Church can live and grow and spread His redemption to all corners of the earth. To that end He gives His Church not only a superhuman *commission*, but also superhuman *power* to carry it out. The great commission is to go and make disciples of all nations. The power is Baptism and teaching, the Word and the Sacraments. The magnitude of that power becomes clearer when the Church hears Him say, "I will give unto thee the keys of the kingdom of heaven" (Matt. 16:19).

"The Keys of the Kingdom!" There is the answer to panic-stricken mankind, sitting with the sizzling firecracker in his hand. "My God, what shall I do with it?" That is the wrong question. Not what *I* will do with it. *I* have done enough. *I*, man, have fanned the flames of hate. *I* have turned nation against nation and given them the power to destroy each other. *I* have furnished the weapons, more ghastly with each generation, by which men have killed millions, and left other millions maimed and crippled, homeless and hopeless, wounded and dying. *I* have left the world in chaos. *I* have torn it up like a cross-word puzzle, and I can't put it together again, because I have lost the pattern. Now, O God, what will *you* do with it?"

How true: man has lost the pattern. God made man in His image. That is the pattern. And when man chooses to follow his own will rather than God's will, then the pattern is destroyed. And then only God can put it together again.

What is this deadly thing which makes man tear up God's pattern for life and try to substitute his own? God calls it *sin*. A short innocent-looking word of three letters, but it is the cause of all man's misery. It is the basic element in that pride—some give it a nicer name, pride of accomplishment—which has driven him on in his scientific pursuits until he has brought the world to zero hour. He has reached the peak, and now he cannot go back. He has created Pinnochio and now he cannot control him. Is there no way out for man? Not until he recognizes and deals with that thing called sin. And until he does, the world will continue to use man's discoveries as weapons of destruction, and with ever increasing effectiveness and fearfulness. And at this point man must see the power which God has given to His Church, the power to deal with sin. It is the greatest power on earth. It reaches into eternity. Beside it the atomic bomb is a two-for-a-cent firecracker. It is the power which Christ gave His Church when He said, "I will give unto thee the keys of the kingdom of heaven." It is the *power of the Keys, the Keys of the kingdom*.

What is it, this power of the Keys? It is the power of God to deal effectively with sin. It is the power to open heaven to a lost sinner who repents, and the power to open hell and close heaven to the impenitent sinner. It is the power to set man right with God, to restore among men God's pattern of life, to bring the will of man into harmony with the will of God. And since it is sin that has disturbed this relation of man to God, it must be a power that can overrule sin. That is exactly the way Jesus defined the power when He gave it to the Church in the person of Peter. "I will give unto thee the keys of the kingdom of heaven: and whatsoever thou shalt bind on earth shall be bound in heaven: and whatsoever thou shalt loose on earth shall be loosed in heaven" (Matt. 16:19).

If that verse stood alone as the only statement on the power of the Keys, there might lie in it a temptation to the Church to abuse this power through misinterpretation of the words of Jesus. When Luther arrived on the scene and began his work of reformation, he found that this very thing had happened. The Pope at Rome, claiming to be the successor of Peter, had twisted this verse into a vicious tool for papal tyranny. He used it as authority for his claim of supremacy over all powers and rulers, temporal and spiritual. Luther challenged the Pope's interpretation and practice in the matter of the Keys. Commenting on this verse of St. Matthew, Luther says, "The Pope takes these letters and goes with them unto the land of the lotus-eaters, and interprets them thus: 'What I do in heaven and earth is right: I have the keys to bind and loose everything.' Yes, even if we had eaten beets! But if one looks at the reasons, one finds that Christ is speaking of the binding and loosing of sin."[3]

Thus Luther puts his finger on the heart of man's problem and therefore also of God's *purpose* in giving

---
[3] *On the Councils and the Churches.* Holman, V. 174.

the power of the Keys to the Church. It is sin that creates man's deepest need and lies at the root of all his misery. That is the thing that has alienated man from God. That is the great enemy from which the Church must save man. And the Keys are the God-given power by which the Church can work that deliverance. But as Luther points out, she must stick to her knitting. This not a power with which to lord it over men in political and economic matters. What misery is caused by the Pope's abuse of this power, says Luther. "Heaven and hell have been opened and shut to whomsoever he would. Whomsoever he would he has taken or left them their body, possessions, honor, land, kingdom, wife, child, house, farm, gold, and everything. And what would the Papacy be if it were not for the abuse of the keys? ... How has not the Pope raged and foamed against emperors, kings, and all the world, yes, against God Himself and His holy word? ... How much war and bloodshed has he caused in all the world."[4]

In tyrannizing temporal rulers, in imposing temporal sanctions, economic boycott and similar things practiced by Rome in our own day Rome is leading the Church into realms where the Lord gave her no authority to rule. She has forgotten that this is a spiritual power to be exercised in spiritual things, more particularly in dealing with man's sin. As Luther says, "The Keys are Keys of the Kingdom of Heaven, into which no one enters except through the forgiveness of sin, and from which no one is excluded except those who are bound because of an impenitent life. Thus the words do not concern St. Peter's power, but the need of miserable sinners, or of proud

---
[4] D. Mart. Luthers Warnung an seine lieben Deutschen. 1531. Erlangen XXV, 44.

sinners; but of these Keys the Pope makes two master-keys to all kings' crowns and treasuries, to all the world's purse, body, honor, and goods."[5]

In limiting this power to the spiritual realm and to dealing with the problem of sin in men, Luther lets our Lord interpret His own words. Matthew 16, which was cited above, is not the whole story of the Keys. It comes again in Matthew 18, where the Lord explains to the Church how to use the Keys in the matter of church discipline. Again in John 20 He tells His disciples what it means to "bind" and "loose." In verse 23 He says, "Whose soever sins ye remit, they are remitted to them; and whose soever sins ye retain, they are retained." Luther comments further on Matthew 16:19. This passage, he says, "can have no other meaning . . . than that our dear Lord and true bishop of our souls has left behind Him the power to bind and loose sins. For there must be discipline and punishment in the Church because of rough and impudent people. Likewise also a comfort and hope for the fallen lest they think their Baptism is lost."[6]

What are the Keys of the Kingdom? Luther persists in answering that question in terms of sin and the Church's dealing with sin. In a sermon on the Feast of St. Peter and St. Paul, his definition is crystal-clear. "The Keys of the Kingdom are nothing else than that one forgives sins to those who believe on Christ and accept the Gospel and opens wide heaven to them: . . . On the other hand, those who do not believe in Christ and do not accept the Gospel, but continue in their sins without improvement, shall not be forgiven their sins, but heaven

---
[5]*On the Councils and the Churches.* Holman, V. 174.
[6]*Wider das Papstthum zu Rom, vom Teufel gestiftet.* 1545. Erlangen XXVI, 178.

shall be closed to them. Such a treasure has the Church, *i.e.*, the group (Haufe) or the assembly (Versammlung) which confesses with Peter that Jesus is the Christ, the Son of the living God."[7]

The Keys of the Kingdom turn both ways. They open and they close the Kingdom. They bind and they loose. They forgive and they retain sins. They save and they damn. And so far from being a human power, they are the power of God. What the Church does with the Keys here on earth is done in heaven. The Church's forgiveness of a sinner is God's forgiveness. The Church's condemnation is God's condemnation. "Whatsoever thou shalt bind on earth shall be bound in heaven: and whatsoever thou shalt loose on earth shall be loosed in heaven" (Matt. 16:19). What the Church says about your sin and what she does about it is done in heaven. God has turned the Keys of the Kingdom over to the Church, and her judgments are His judgments. Luther paraphrases the words of our Lord on this point: Christ speaks to His Church and says, "Those whom you on earth declare damned and the devil's own, those I will in heaven declare to be such. For what is bound on earth through you, that shall also be bound in heaven by me. . . . There shall be one binding, on earth below and in heaven above. Here God binds Himself by the judgment of the Holy Christian Church, when rightly used, so that the Church's judgment is God's own judgment."[8] Luther, too, meets the hardened, wise-cracking individual, whom we know so well, who says, "Nobody is going to tell me what to believe. I have learned enough to know in my own heart

---
[7] *Predigt am Tage St. Petri und Pauli, über Matt. 16:13-19*. Erlangen VI, 296.
[8] *Predigten über etliche Kapitel des Evangelisten Matthäi*. Erlangen XLIV, 88.

how I'm going to be saved, even if my pastor does excommunicate me." Luther tells him, "You can depend on it, the Lord Christ will not judge otherwise than as the Christian Church judges."⁹

Luther finds the Church in great confusion regarding the power of the Keys. People do not understand the *purpose* of the Keys, and so they either fear them or despise them. The cause of this, says Luther, is that the Pope, besides stretching the power to things temporal, has made it a law, rather than a comforting Gospel treatment of the sinner. Make a law out of the Keys and you give the Pope and the clergy a whip with which to lash terrified sinners into obedience-or-else. The Pope, says Luther, makes a law of this power, to exercise as he will. One commandment after another he gives, and whoever does not keep it shall be excommunicated (banned). Whoever keeps it shall have abundant indulgence. Keep your St. Francis' Day, eat no meat on Friday, make your pilgrimages, or the papal bann will smite you.¹⁰ This power to threaten and frighten, the Pope then extends beyond the spiritual and uses it to intimidate emperors and to beat temporal rulers into submission. "The Keys are not to bind and loose sins (as the Lord says), but the power and the right which is given the Pope over all earthly kingdoms and the Kingdom of heaven."¹¹ Confusing the temporal with the spiritual power, the state with the Church, "the Pope's bann is an imperial punishment, such as exile, that is a worldly bann, where a man is outlawed. To us is not given the rule over bodily matters. The spiritual bann, which Christ preaches and wields,

---
⁹*Ibid.*, p. 89.
¹⁰*Ibid.*, p. 99.
¹¹*Wider das Papstthum zu Rom, vom Teufel gestiftet. 1545.* Erlangen XXVI, 181.

belongs to us."[12] This gives the Church no rights in the emperor's realm. The emporor can judge a thief, but he cannot damn a soul.

The difference between Luther and Rome in the doctrine of the Keys is a basic difference. It runs all the way through their respective doctrinal systems. With Rome the emphasis is preeminently Law—authority, obedience, fear, submission. With Luther it is Gospel, which is the *opus proprium*, the proper work, of God, while Law is the *opus alienum*, the foreign work. So in the doctrine of the Keys, the purpose of the power is to save the sinner, and that whether you bind or loose him. Now, it is true, the binding is a matter of Law, and the loosing a matter of Gospel. Condemnation—forgiveness is the formula. But behind both lies the redeeming love of God reaching out through the arms of Mother Church to save the sinner. And the whole concern is to deal with the man's sin. No power-politics, no interference by the Church in the affairs of the state, belong here. "God has given His Church the Keys for comfort." The Pope, says Luther, uses them to threaten and frighten, to destroy and oppress.[13] "The Keys and such power to bind and loose are given the Apostles and saints not to rule over the churches, but only for the good of the sinners. For where there is no sin, there the Keys and their office are not needed. . . . Hence it is not any worldly power by which the bishops may boast and rule, but a spiritual power given for the good and health of sinners, that they may seek and find it from the bishops and churches, as often as they have need, in order that the sinner may

---
[12]*Predigten über etliche Kapitel des Evangelisten Matthäi.* Erlangen XLIV, 86.
[13]*Ibid.,* 86.

be saved, and not that the bishops may be lords and knights."[14]

Even in binding the sinner in his sin, the Church is not driving him down to hell. She is trying to bring him to repentance. Christ's purpose is "to deliver the sinner from his sins, and He aims at nothing else with His binding than that the sinner's conscience might be set free from sins. For He punishes and binds the sinner, in order that he shall forsake sin, repent of it and shun it. Hence such binding may be called a deliverance of the conscience and a help against sin."[15]

THE KEY OF "BINDING": EXCOMMUNICATION

What has Protestantism, what has Luther's own Church, done with this key, the power to bind an impenitent sinner in his sin? How rare it is to see this power exercised among us. Where is excommunication? Where is church discipline? We cannot appeal to Luther to defend our laxity. Luther finds that in his day the power has been distorted and abused. It is no longer used to deal summarily with sin, but rather is it applied as a temporal and political power. And he cries out for a restoration of the right exercise of the Keys. "We must restore the excommunication . . . so that when we see a usurer, an adulterer, etc., we say to him, 'Do you hear, it is the cry that you are such and such, therefore go not to the Sacrament, abstain from Baptism, lead no bride to the church'; summa, forbid him everything which is the Church." But this is to be limited to spiritual things. We must not do as the Pope does, apply it to physical things,

---

[14] *Wider das Papstthum zu Rom, vom Teufel gestiftet. 1545.* Erlangen XXVI, 164.
[15] *D. Martin Luthers Schrift von den Schlüsseln.* Walch XIX, 1125.

like barring him forcibly from the market, and the like. And mark this, he shall not be forbidden to go to church to hear preaching, for there through the preaching he will learn where he has failed.[16]

The power of thus dealing with the recalcitrant sinner is based on Matt. 16:19, "Whatsoever thou shalt bind on earth . . ." "You learn here that the Lord Christ has established such a fine regiment in the Church that He and it shall have the power in case of public sins and vices to bind and bann people through the Word."[17] So when the Church finds a man who "wants to be called a Christian, and yet continue in open sin," him shall the Church bind according to the Word of God.[18] And if he will not hear you or the Church, let him, as our Lord says, "be unto thee as an heathen man and a publican" (Matt. 18:17). "Give him this sentence and judgment, that he is cut off from the Church, deprived of all grace which God has given the Church and whatever more the Christians have. If he despises such and does not yield, shall I take him by the neck? No, that is for the emperor to do. . . . Let the emperor rule his belly; you rule the soul, preacher."[19]

Luther has no magic formula for excommunication, nor is he much concerned about the technique of the thing. Only let the unrepentant open sinner know that he has by his sinning cut himself off from the Church and the fellowship of the saints. For this is a fellowship of believers, a Communion of Saints, who believe in Christ

---
[16]*Tischreden.* Erlangen LIX, 180.
[17]*Predigten über etliche Kapitel des Evangelisten Matthäi.* Erlangen XLIV 87.
[18]*Ibid.*, 104.
[19]*Ibid.*, 86.

and who long for the forgiveness which He offers them in the Church. The impenitent excommunicates himself, says Luther. "Extortioners, drunkards, revellers, whoremongers, criminals, and blasphemers we do not excommunicate; they excommunicate themselves, yes, they are already in it above their ears. They despise the Word of God, they come to no church, hear no preaching, do not attend the Sacrament. Very well, if they will not be Christians, let them be heathen. . . . And if they want to take the goods and income of the pastors and grab everything for themselves, the pastor shall not give them absolution or the Sacrament, they shall not come to, or stand sponsors at, any Baptism, nor shall they come to an honorable wedding or a burial; they shall be regarded as the heathen they have chosen to be. And when they die, no pastor, no vicar, shall come to them; and when they are dead, let the hangman drag them out of the city to the extortioner's grave (Schindergrube), there shall no student, no vicar come; since they want to be heathen, we will regard them as heathen."[20]

In "A Treatise Concerning the Bann" of 1570 one is particularly struck with the Gospel emphasis which Luther puts on excommunication. It is only a parental chastisement whereby Mother Church seeks to win the erring brother back to the truth and the right way of life. Excommunication is discussed as the counterpart of communion. The fellowship of believers is called communion, which is also used to designate the Sacrament. The latter is also "a sign of the communion of all saints." And the peculiar function of the bann is to "deprive guilty Christians of the holy Sacrament and forbid it to them."

---

[20] *Tischreden.* Erlangen LIX, 179.

Excommunication, then, describes the exclusion from this fellowship.[21]

There is, however, a twofold fellowship. One is the inner spiritual fellowship in the Communion of Saints. From this fellowship of faith no one can be excluded by an act of Pope or any other creature. Only God has authority here. "This fellowship no bann can touch or affect, but only the unbelief or sin of the person himself; by these he can excommunicate himself, and thus separate himself from the grace, life and salvation of the fellowship."[22] The other is "an outward, bodily and visible fellowship, by which one is admitted to the holy Sacrament." From this fellowship a Pope or bishop can exclude a person because of his sin. This is called the "lesser bann." But the bann goes beyond this and "forbids even burial, selling, trading, all association and fellowship with men, finally, as they say, even fire and water, and this is known as the greater bann."[23] Both are instituted by Christ in Matthew 18.[24]

Over against the reckless abuse of the bann Luther emphasizes that it is serious business to exercise this power and a terrible thing to make a mistake in excommunicating a sinner unjustly. The treatment is more dangerous for the one who exercises it than for the one who receives it. For if an innocent man is unjustly put under the bann, it harms him not at all, except to cause him to suffer the loss of outward fellowship. For he remains in the fellowship of Christ and all the saints. In such case he shall endure the bann patiently and heartily continue to desire the Sacrament until he die, if the bann

---

[21] *A Treatise Concerning the Bann.* 1520. Holman, II. 37.
[22] *Ibid.*, pp. 37, 38.
[23] *Ibid.*
[24] *Ibid.*, p. 39.

is not lifted. For the Church cannot by excommunication "deliver a soul to Satan and deprive it of the intercession and of all the good works of the Church." The bann, in such case, can only exclude from the outward association in the Church, and "there remains a real participation in all the possessions and intercessions of the Church, together with all the benefits of the Sacrament."[25]

Where the bann is rightly understood, it is used to convict the impenitent sinner, to admonish and chastise him, "whereby the one under the bann should recognize that he himself has delivered his soul unto Satan by his transgression and sin, and has deprived himself of the fellowship of all the saints and of Christ." Here again we see Luther's glorious conception of the Church as the Holy Mother reaching out with the tender love of Christ to bring back one of her straying children. And when she has to put such a one under the bann it is as if she is saying, "Behold, thou hast done this or that, whereby thou hast delivered thy soul unto the devil, deserved God's wrath, and deprived thyself of all Christian fellowship; thou art fallen under the inward spiritual bann in the sight of God and art unwilling to cease or to return. So, then, I put thee also outwardly under the bann in the sight of men, and to thy shame I deprive thee of the Sacrament and of fellowship with men, until thou come to thyself and bring back thy soul."[26]

Thus the bann is to be used and received as "a medicine and not a poison."[27] It is not meant to harm or destroy, "but seeks and finds the ruined and condemned

---
[25] *Ibid.*, p. 40.
[26] *Ibid.*, p. 41.
[27] *Ibid.*, p. 43.

soul for the purpose of bringing it back. For all chastisement is for the correction of sin; the bann is simply a chastisement and motherly correction ... ordained solely to restore the inward spiritual fellowship when justly laid, or to deepen it when unjustly imposed.... For the bann can be nothing else than a kind motherly scourge applied to the body and temporal possessions, by which no one is cast into hell, but rather drawn out of it, and freed from condemnation unto salvation."

Before closing this important treatise, Luther takes time to point out the proper object of the Church's excommunication. "The bann should be applied not only to heretics and schismatics, but to all who are guilty of open sin, as we have shown above from St. Paul, who commands that the railer, extortioner, fornicator and drunkard be put under the bann."[28] Then he adds a touch that might well be aimed at the Church of the twentieth century. "But in our day such sinners are left in peace, especially if they are big-wigs." Now let the Church revive the use of this power, or this ministry, as Luther prefers to call it. Let them use it strictly in the realm of the spiritual. For "the spiritual powers should be concerned with the Word of God, with sin, and with the devil, in order to bring souls to God."[29] Let the Word of God have free course and the Word will do its work and accomplish its purpose. Even the sinner under the bann must not be excluded from the Church till after the Gospel has been read and the sermon preached. For "the Word of God should remain free to everyone."[30]

---
[28]*Ibid.*, p. 53.
[29]*Ibid.*, p. 54.
[30]*Ibid.*, p. 54.

THE KEY OF "LOOSING": FORGIVENESS

If we want to speak of *two* Keys, one for "binding" and one for "loosing," we must not forget that they have *one purpose*. While the one Key applies the Law and the other the Gospel, the purpose of both is to *save*. Hence we may say that they both have a "Gospel purpose." This is only another way of bringing out that great principle of Luther's when he says that the Law is the "foreign" work of God, the Gospel is His "proper" work. Luther says, God's proper work is "the doing of righteousness, peace, mercy, truth, meekness, goodness, joy, salvation. . . . He cannot, however, approach this, His proper work, unless He adopts a work alien and contrary to Himself. . . . His alien work is to make men sinners, unrighteous, liars, sad, fools, lost—not that He Himself makes them so in truth, but since they are so . . . God uses this work so that He may show them to be so, so that they may become in their own eyes what they are in the eyes of God. Thus, since He cannot make any righteous save those who are unrighteous, He is obliged before His proper work of justification to labor at an alien work to make men sinners."[31] Behind it all lies the eternal Gospel principle that God "will have all men to be saved, and to come unto the knowledge of the truth" (I Tim. 2:4). To effect this salvation God uses primarily the Gospel. This alone can save, since it alone can produce faith and create life. But God also uses the Law to show a man his sin and thus prepare him for the coming of the Gospel of forgiveness.

In that way the "binding" Key, or excommunication, is used. Its purpose is to terrify a sinner by showing him

---
[31] *Sermo in Die S. Thomae*. W. I, 112.

the seriousness of his sin and thus driving him to repentance. Thus it has become a gracious preparatory work until the Church can apply the other Key and offer him forgiveness through the Gospel. For the "loosing" Key is to be applied only to troubled consciences, and by no means to those that are secure and unconcerned about sin. The power to use the Keys to forgive sin, says Luther, was given the Church "in order that poor sinful consciences may find comfort when they are 'loosed,' or absolved by man; and the words apply only to sinful, timid, troubled consciences, and are intended to strengthen them, if they but believe."[32]

Luther's loving concern for souls stands out in this doctrine just as it does in his teaching of justification by faith and in his whole doctrine of *grace alone*. "The Keys," he says, "is not a power, but a service. . . . Hence Christ has ordained . . . that the clergy should not thereby serve themselves, but only us."[33] Christians should be made aware that in the Church lies for them this great source of comfort. For "Christ has given the apostles and the Christian Church the Keys and left this glorious text (Mt. 16:18-19) behind Him for the comfort of the Church. On this foundation stands the holy Christian Church. . . . When among Christians one sins and wants to turn and know whether God will be merciful or not, and wants to live and die on that, he has this comfort in the church: . . . 'Whatsoever thou shalt loose on earth shall be loosed in heaven.' "[34]

The main purpose of the Keys, then, and the specific

---

[32] *The Papacy at Rome.* Holman, I. 378.
[33] *Sermon vom Sacrament der Busse.* Erlangen XX, 187.
[34] *Predigt über etliche Kapitel des Evangelisten Matthäi.* Erlangen XLIV 93.

purpose of the "loosing" Key is to apply Christ's atonement to the sinner in terms of forgiveness. It is not only to open the door to the Kingdom of God, but to actually lead him into the Kingdom. "The Keys of Christ serve and help the sinner into heaven and into eternal life; for He Himself calls them the Keys of the Kingdom of heaven, namely, that they close the heaven to the hardened sinner, but open it to the penitent one. Therefore there must lie hidden in the Keys of Christ His blood, death and resurrection, with which He has opened the Kingdom of Heaven and gives the poor sinner through the Keys what He has procured through His blood. So the office of the Keys is a high and divine office which helps the soul from sin and death to grace and life, and gives him righteousness without any merit of works, alone through the forgiveness of sins."[35]

THE ADMINISTRATION OF THE KEYS

We have already noted that according to Luther the Keys were given, not to Peter in his person, but to Peter as the representative of the Church. Hence Luther declares in the "Smalcald Articles" that "the Keys are an office and power given by Christ *to the Church* for binding and loosing sin."[36] And this is no mere static thing which the Church has. It includes both the power and the use of it. "The Keys belong to the entire congregation of Christians, and to everyone who is a member of that congregation: and that not alone as regards the power, but also the use in every imaginable case."[37]

---

[35] *D. Mart. Luthers Schrift von den Schlüsseln.* Walch 19, 1126.
[36] *Vom Gebet des Herrn oder Vater Unser.* Walch X, 1846f.
[37] Art VII. "The Smalcald Articles." *Concordia Triglotta,* p. 493.

The power of the Keys is exercised through the Word and Sacraments. There is no other way. They are the only Means of Grace. Forgiveness comes only through Word and Sacraments. They alone turn the Key to the Kingdom of God. It is through the Gospel that the atonement of Christ so burns itself into a sinner's soul that he cries, "I know that my Redeemer liveth." In the Gospel he has heard the sure voice of God saying, "Thine iniquity is taken away, and thy sin is purged" (Isa. 60:7). Luther drives the troubled sinner back, always back to the Word. "The Lord our God made forgiveness of sins contingent on no work that we might perform, but on the great work which Christ accomplished when He died for the world, and for our benefit arose from the dead. The application of this His work He makes through the Word which He entrusted to the apostles, to the ministers of the Gospel, yea to every Christian, authorizing them to declare unto all who seek it the remission of sins. Thus we have pointed out to us the only way in which we can surely find remission of sins, and in the Word we are sure to find this remission. If we seek it not there, our sins will be retained, do what we may; for . . . there is no remission except in the Word of Christ."[38]

Who is to bring this Word of forgiveness to the sinner? Luther answered that in the previous quotation by saying that the Word was "entrusted to the apostles, to the *ministers* of the Gospel, yea to *every Christian.*" Hence the power of the Keys, which was given to the Church, is exercised:

---
[38] *Am Sonntag Quasi modo geniti.* W. LII, 273. Tr. by Uuras Saarnivaara, *The Power of the Keys,* p. 33f. Hancock, Mich.: Finnish Lutheran Book Concern, 1944.

1. by every Christian because of the spiritual priesthood of believers;
2. by the office of the ministry.

It was in that critical period around 1519, when Luther was fighting it out on the line of *authority* with Eck and others, that he came to see the significance of the New Testament doctrine of the *universal priesthood of all believers*. We have seen how Eck drove him to the epoch-making statement that a General Council could err and had erred. With his rejection of the papal claim to the Keys as the successor of Peter, Luther had thus cast off the traditional ecclesiastical authority, whereby the Pope and the priesthood had lorded it over the thinking and the faith of the laity. The people in the pews had not been permitted to think for themselves theologically or religiously. They were not invited or allowed to search the Scriptures themselves. The Church was the infallible interpreter of the Bible. The Pope was the keeper of the Keys. When Luther challenged these principles it appeared that he had opened the flood gates to chaos. Was it not an invitation to a field day of sectarianism? It would have been if Luther had not given a positive answer to the problems he thus had raised.

Luther's answer was that the Word of God was its own interpreter, and that God had not given its interpretation into the hands of any man or organization of men. Further, he declared that Christ gave the Keys to the Church, the Communion of Saints. But his thinking was realistic enough to see that this power must be exercised in the world. And here he called in the New Testament idea of the spiritual priesthood of believers. In his "Open Letter to the Christian Nobility," he rejected the Roman idea of a "spiritual estate" of Pope, bishops, priests, and monks, which held a position above the "temporal estate" to which belonged the farmer and the artisan and everybody else. Here was an Old Testament pattern of priesthood holding a rank far above the ordinary layman. It was a feudal class-society, of which the New Testament knows nothing. Luther told the people not to take this distinction seriously, because according to Scripture "all Christians are truly of the 'spiritual estate,' and there is among them no difference at all other than that of office, as Paul says in I Cor. 12: We are all one body, yet every member has its own work, whereby it serves every other, all because we have one Baptism, one Gospel, one faith, and are all alike Christians; for Baptism, Gospel and faith alone make us 'spiritual' and a Christian people."[39] We are all consecrated priests by Baptism, as I Peter 2:9 says, "Ye are a royal priesthood, an holy nation." And Rev. 5:10 declares, "Thou hast made us . . . kings and priests."

Luther insists that this breaks down all class distinctions in the Church. He says in 1521, "There is in reality no difference between the bishops, elders and priests and the laity, no one being distinguished from other Christians, except that he has an office, which is committed to him, to preach the Word of God and to administer the Sacraments."[40] Luther appeals repeatedly to Peter, and declares that he "says that in the New Testament there are no special priests, but that all Christians are priests, typified by those priests" (Old Testament priests).[41]

---
[39] Holman, II. 66.
[40] *D. Martin Luthers Schrift vom Miszbrauch der Messe.* Walch XIX, p. 1340.
[41] "*Kirchenpostille.*" Walch XII, 1889.

This is more than a doctrine and a theory. As a member of the royal priesthood of believers every Christian must feel his responsibility as a priest. "Do you ask, Wherein consists the priesthood of believers?...Answer: The very same of which we have been speaking, namely, teaching, sacrificing and praying. If we have become Christians . . . then we have also received the right and power to teach and confess the Word that he gives us before all, every one according to his calling and place. For although we do not all occupy a public office and calling, yet every believer may and should teach, instruct, exhort, comfort, rebuke his neighbor through the Word of God, whenever and wherever that may be needed."[42]

Jesus Christ is Himself the High Priest. He alone carries out fully the work of the priest. God established the pattern of the priesthood in the Old Testament. His work was to teach the Word of God, to sacrifice, and to pray. And it all had meaning only with reference to the coming Messiah. His teaching was concerned with the Law, which only the Messiah could fulfill. His sacrifices were only types of the great sacrifice of the Lamb of God and were efficacious for the forgiveness of sins only through faith in Him. His prayers, too, found access to the Father only through the promised Son.

But with Christ came the fulfillment of all this. He fulfilled the Law. He was the sacrifice that God Himself offered for the sins of the world. And He Himself is the Intercessor and the Mediator for all the prayers of all God's children. God has put all things in His hands. Aaron must withdraw and say, "I am indeed a high priest [by God's command], but my priesthood continues only

---

[42]*Der CX Psalm . . . gepredigt und ausgelegt. 1539.* Erlangen XL, 172.

until this Lord come. Now that He is come, I, with all others, must accept and honor Him as the true High Priest."[43]

In this "Exposition of the 110th Psalm" Luther then goes on to demolish the idea that Christ passed this priesthood on to Peter and through him to the bishop of Rome. On the contrary, He gave this New Testament priesthood, not to an order or a class, but to the Church, the Communion of Saints. And He anointed every believer a priest in holy Baptism. This New Testament priest has one preëminent duty: to proclaim the Gospel of forgiveness to men. "The true priestly office is to preach the Gospel, which means nothing else than an open preaching of God's grace and forgiveness of sins."[44] The responsibility for spreading the Gospel of forgiveness rests upon every Christian, since every one is a priest. As Luther so often said, however, and as we must constantly remember, that does not give every Christian the right to claim the office of the public ministry. But here again the principle is clear and consistent in Luther, that the Keys of the Kingdom were given to the Church.

This Gospel is proclaimed and the Key is turned through absolution, through preaching, and through the Sacraments. Absolution itself is a broad term, and it means the application of the Gospel to the sinner, whether given by a friend, or by a pastor in the Confessional or through preaching and administering of the Sacraments. It offers the sinner forgiveness and bestows what it offers. "Whatsoever thou shalt loose on earth shall be loosed in heaven" (Matt. 16:19)

---

[43] *Ibid.*, p. 137f.
[44] *Ibid.*, p. 152.

Because of the universal priesthood of believers, every Christian has the right and the privilege of declaring to a troubled sinner the forgiveness of his sins. Here is a teaching of tremendous comfort, which Luther restored to the common man. The boundless love of Christ is too big to be shut up behind the exclusive doors of a priestly order. Christ is living and active in His Church, and His forgiving love flows through the whole Body and every member in it. It must live where two or three are assembled, "in order that they may speak comfort and forgiveness of sins to one another."[45] Christ is so rich in forgiveness that He literally "chucks all corners full of forgiveness of sins, so that they [we] may find forgiveness . . . not only in the congregation, but at home, in the field, in the garden, and when one meets another he shall find comfort and salvation." When I am sad and troubled, no matter what . . . hour it is, "if I cannot at all times find preaching in the church, and my brother or neighbor come to me, I shall bring my complaint to him and ask him for comfort: what he gives me of comfort shall then be yea and amen with God in heaven."

This is a mutual affair, and I have a responsibility to help my neighbor in love as well as to seek his help in my trouble. Luther, always practical and helpful in the way of the Christian life, says I shall reach out a helping hand to my suffering brother in anguish of conscience and say, "Dear friend, dear brother, why are you troubled? It is not the will of God that you should have a single sorrow. God has given His Son to die for you, that you should not be sad, but happy. So be of good courage. You will do God a pleasing service thereby." Then, says

---

[45]*Predigten über etliche Kapitel des Evangelisten Matthäi.* Erlangen XLIV, 107f.

Luther, "get down on your knees together and pray an *Our Father*. It will surely be heard in heaven, for Christ says: I am in the midst of you. He does not say: I see it, I hear it, or I will come to you, but I am already there. So when you comfort me, and I you, and we do it for our mutual help and salvation, then I must believe you, and you me, that God our heavenly Father wishes to give us what we seek and need. How could our Lord more richly care for us?"[46]

The second duty of the priest, says Luther, is *sacrifice*. Here again Christ is the true High Priest. He alone can offer the sufficient sacrifice for the sins of the world. "Christ is the only priest, sent of God, who can reconcile us to God and gain forgiveness.... He has made the sacrifice in obedience to God's command."[47] Likewise, every Christian, born a priest in Baptism, shall offer priestly sacrifices. Not that he can thereby make or offer sacrifice for sin. Only Christ can do that, and has done it. But he is to offer sacrifices of praise and honor to God. It is what St. Paul speaks of in Romans 12:1, beseeching the Christians to present their bodies "a living sacrifice, holy, acceptable unto God." "Such an offering," says Luther, "consists in cross and suffering. For if a man will confess Christ, he will have to risk property and honor, body and life.... These are the right sacrifices which please God and are a sweet incense. For they honor God and give the people a good example."[48]

Together with preaching and sacrifice, the priest's work is to pray. Our great High Priest has ascended to the right hand of the Father, "that through His interces-

---
[46] *Ibid.*, 108.
[47] *Der CX Psalm ... gepredigt und ausgelegt.* Erlangen XL, 155.
[48] *Ibid.*, 173.

sion He may keep us eternally in the grace of God, give us power and victory over the terrors of sin, the devil, and the world, and over the temptations of the flesh. And He not only prays for us, but grants us that we persevere and that we can ourselves pray to God; He bears our petitions before God and assures us that for His sake such prayer will please God and be heard."[49]

Through the mediation of this intercessory priesthood of Christ, every Christian is ordained to this high honor. When even "a young baptized child, morning, evening, and at the table, says his *Ten Commandments, Creed,* and *Our Father,* that is true prayer, heard of God; for he prays as a Christian and a priest, born and ordained through Christ."[50]

It should be said again that when Luther is speaking of our Christian activity as priests, his emphasis is always primarily on the proclamation of the Gospel of forgiveness. This is not only the *opus proprium,* the proper work, of God. It is the *opus proprium* of every Christian in his status of priest. For the Gospel is the great gift God has given His Church, the power to forgive sin and to save the lost. "Behold, such is the authority given through this office of the apostles to the Church. . . . But who can express what an unspeakable, mighty and blessed comfort it is that a human being can with one word open heaven and lock hell to a fellow mortal? For in this Kingdom of grace Christ has founded through His resurrection, we do indeed nothing else than open our mouth and say, I forgive thee thy sins, not on my ac-

---
[49] *Ibid.,* 156f.
[50] *Ibid.,* 174.

count, nor by my power, but in the place of and in the name of Jesus Christ."[51]

Luther now makes his transition from the priesthood of all believers to the office of the public ministry and shows the relation of both and the distinction between the two. No attempt will be made to give a thorough analysis of Luther's doctrine of the ministry; but its relation to the priesthood of believers should at least be clarified.

There is an *office of the ministry*, instituted by God. For "he gave some, apostles; and some, prophets; and some, evangelists; and some, pastors and teachers; for the perfecting of the saints, for the work of the ministry, for the edifying of the body of Christ" (Eph. 4:11-12). Luther says that some are chosen *immediately* by Christ for the ministry. Such are the prophets and apostles, "who are chosen, not by men nor through a man, but through Jesus Christ and God the Father." Then there are those who are chosen *mediately* by God through men. "Such are the disciples of the apostles and all, even to the end of the world, who enter the ministry of preaching rightfully in the place of the apostles, as bishops and priests. And these cannot exist without the former, from which they have their beginning."[52]

With all his emphasis on the priesthood of believers, Luther still maintains a high regard for the ministry as an office instituted by God. "I trust that the believers and all who want to be called Christians know well that the spiritual estate [geistliche Stand] is instituted ... by God, not with gold or silver, but with the precious blood and

---
[51] Erlangen XI, 392.
[52] *Auslegung des Evangelii am Tage Andreä*. Walch XI, 2553.

bitter death of His own Son, our Lord Jesus Christ. For verily from His wounds . . . flow the Sacraments, and He has ordained that there is this office throughout the world to preach, baptize, loose, bind, give the Sacrament, comfort, warn, admonish, with the Word of God, and whatever else belongs to the office of soul-curate."[53] This is not a contradiction to his statement in the "Address to the Nobility," where he rejects the idea of a spiritual estate which is superior to the laity, a separate class and order. He therefore adds in this "Sermon on Keeping the Children in School": "I do not mean the present spiritual estate in cloisters and chapters. . . . I mean the estate which has the office of preaching and the service of the Word and Sacraments, which gives the Spirit and salvation . . . the office of pastor, teacher, preacher, reader, priest . . . sexton, schoolmaster, and whatever else belongs to such offices and persons, which estate the Scripture extols and praises."[54]

While every Christian is a priest, everyone may not arrogate to himself this office of the public ministry of Word and Sacraments. Luther interprets I Cor. 4:1 ("Let a man so account of us, as of the ministers of Christ") and says that Paul "has reference to the ministry that is an office. All Christians serve God but all are not in office."[55] All priests should remember that they were once laymen like the rest, and they were only chosen to the office by the congregation that they should preach. "For there is only one distinction outwardly by reason of the office to which one from the congregation has been chosen."[56]

---
[53]*Ein Sermon oder Predigt, dasz man solle Kinder zur Schule halten. 1530.* Walch X, 488f.
[54]*Loc. cit.*
[55]*Sermon on the Third Sunday in Advent.* Lenker VII, 65.
[56]*Auslegung der ersten Epistel St. Petri, 1523.* Walch IX, 702f.

Luther's interpretation of the spiritual priesthood of all believers and its relation to the ministerial office was unquestionably a radical departure from the traditional conception of the priesthood. Again he seemed to invite disrespect for the office. History has proved that this was by no means the result. The office of the ministry is to this day highly esteemed in the Lutheran Church. Where it is not, the reason lies not in Luther's teaching, but in the aberrations of later movements. For Luther guarded the doctrine very carefully in two ways. In the first place he extolled the office as an institution of God, undergirded with blessed promises. In the second place he insisted that no one had the right to claim the office unless he was regularly called by a congregation. "Every Christian has and exercises such a priestly work. But above that is the common [gemeine] office, which publicly carries on the teaching, to which belong pastors and preachers. For they cannot all expect to carry on the office in the congregation; it is not becoming to baptize and celebrate the Sacrament in every house. Therefore certain ones must be chosen and ordained, sent to preach and exercise themselves in the Scripture, to perform the office of teaching and to defend the same; thus to administer the Sacrament for the congregation, so they will know who has been baptized, and everything will be done in order."[57] The Church would be slow in coming if every man preached to the other and everything was done without order. "The priestly office is no such thing, but a common public office for those who are all priests, *i.e.*, Christians."

Luther is not interested in tearing down established

---

[57] *Der CX Psalm . . . gepredigt und ausgelegt. 1539.* Erlangen XL, 174.

traditions that promote order and are not contrary to Scripture. He does not oppose the arrangement whereby there are bishops and other offices among the clergy. This is all a part of good order, which the apostle demands. But bishops must not be held up as a superior class, holding their special authority over the other clergy by divine right. They hold that superior authority only by ecclesiastical right. By divine right they are all equally priests or pastors. So that when a bishop carries out his office, he does it by the authority of the Church and of the general priesthood of all believers. "Therefore, when the bishop consecrates it is the same thing as if he, in the place and stead of the whole congregation, all of whom have like power, were to take one out of their number and charge him to use this power for the others; just as though ten brothers, all king's sons and equal heirs, were to choose one of themselves to rule the inheritance for them all—they would all be kings and equal in power, though one of them would be charged with the duty of ruling."[58]

Luther's classic illustration at this point is well known. "If a little group of pious Christian laymen were taken captive and set down in a wilderness, and had among them no priest consecrated by a bishop, and if there in the wilderness they were to agree in choosing one of themselves, married or unmarried, and were to charge him with the office of baptizing, saying mass, absolving and preaching, such a man would be as truly a priest as though all bishops and popes had consecrated him."

The normal thing is for the bishop to consecrate a

---

[58] *An Open Letter to the Christian Nobility of the German Nation.* Holman II. 67.

priest which the congregation has chosen. Where there is no emergency, "no bishop ought to appoint anyone without the consent, choice, and call of the congregation; it is his duty rather to confirm the man whom the congregation has elected and called. If the bishop does not confirm him, he is none the less confirmed by virtue of the call of the congregation. For neither Titus nor Timothy nor Paul appointed any priest unless he was chosen and called by the congregation."[59] This puts the bishop on the same level as every pastor, except for the authority the Church has given him to supervise, ordain, etc. Luther will have nothing of the Roman idea which regards "the estate of bishop and pope as superior to the office of preacher."[60] For, he says, the office of preaching "is in truth the highest office of all, on which all other offices depend, and from which they follow. . . . Therefore the man who has committed to him the office of preaching has committed to him the highest office in the Christian Church." He repeats the great thought that the "highest office" in the Church is "that of the Word."[61]

Just as he laid it on the conscience of the whole priesthood of believers, so Luther laid upon the ministry the one paramount duty of proclaiming the Gospel of forgiveness to men through the atonement of Jesus Christ. For this power of the Keys to forgive sin is the great treasure of the Church. And "such treasure the Christian Church distributes not only in the Word through absolution and public preaching, but also through Baptism and in the Supper of the Lord Christ."[62]

---

[59] *The right and power of a Christian congregation or community to judge all teaching and to call, appoint, and dismiss teachers.* Holman IV, 82.
[60] *Ibid.*, 84.
[61] *Loc. cit.*
[62] *Op. cit.* Erlangen VI, 296.

As pointed out previously, absolution is the declaration and bestowal of forgiveness, whether it be done in preaching, in confession, or in the Sacrament. For, says Luther, "the Keys of the Church are not to be distinguished, but their use is manifold. The Gospel, when publicly proclaimed and preached, is the public common absolution, which declares and offers forgiveness of sins to all who are penitent. But auricular confession is the special absolution, whereby one is individually absolved of sin or bound."[63]

Because to Luther the Christian life was a constant tension between human sin and divine forgiveness, private confession and absolution was of paramount importance in the Church. For here the Keys of the Kingdom are used by the Church to bring forgiveness and comfort to the individual sinner. The same grace of God which is offered generally through the preaching of the Gospel is here offered to the individual. And it is this personal treatment which the troubled sinner needs so keenly. Luther found he could not live without this comfort and be happy. "I will let no man take private confession from me, and would not give it up for all the treasures in the world, since I know what comfort and strength it has given me. No one knows what private confession can do for him except he who has struggled much with the devil. Yea, the devil would have slain me long ago, if the confession had not sustained me. For there are many doubts which a man cannot solve and understand himself. When he now is in such doubt and does not know how to get out of it, he takes a brother

---

[63] *Tischreden.* Erlangen LIX, 179.

aside and tells him his trouble, complains of his shortcomings, his unbelief and his sins, and asks for comfort and counsel. For what does it matter if he humble himself a little before a neighbor and take shame on himself?"[64]

Luther sees the "word of forgiveness" living in the Church. And every Christian should know that it is there at his disposal at all times and for his comfort. Thus the "spiritual priesthood of believers" becomes a reality, when every Christian is a priest, ready to bring this word of comfort to his brother. So does the "Communion of Saints" walk out of the dogmatics book and become a very life-principle in the Church. For there we share the life-giving Word and Sacraments together with all the spiritual blessings that lie in them, Christian to Christian offering the sure word of forgiveness and the comfort of the Gospel. This is our life in the Body of Christ. "Therefore let every Christian when the devil attacks him and suggests that he is a great sinner, and that he must be lost and condemned, etc., not long contend with him or remain alone, but go to or call his pastor, or any other good friend, lay his difficulty before him, and seek counsel and comfort from him, and remain firm in that which Christ here declares: 'Whose soever sins ye remit, they are remitted unto them,' and as He says in another place: 'Where two or more are gathered together in my name, there am I in the midst of them,' and whatever this person says to him in the name of Christ from the Scriptures, let him believe it, and according to his faith it shall be done unto him."[65]

Luther's pattern here is very evident. He is concerned

---

[64]*Predigten des Jahres 1522.* 8. W. X, pt. 3, 61f.
[65]Church Postil. *Die dritte predigt am Sonntag Quasi modo geniti.* W. XLIX, 147; Lenker XI, 394.

with sinners only. The great need of the sinner is forgiveness. That forgiveness is to be found only in one place, that is in the Word of God and the accompanying Sacrament. But Luther directs the sinner, not only to his own Bible; he tells him that the Church stands ready to declare this word of forgiveness to him and to apply the Word to his particular need. Whether he goes to the minister, which is the normal practice, or he goes to another Christian, it is the *Word* which they must give him; no word of their own, but the Word of God, the Gospel of Jesus Christ. "The Lord our God made forgiveness of sins contingent on no work that we might perform, but on the great work which Christ accomplished when He died for the world, and for our benefit arose from the dead. The application of this His work He makes through the Word which He entrusted to the apostles, to the ministers of the Gospel, yea, to every Christian, authorizing them to declare unto all who seek it the remission of sins. Thus we have pointed out to us the only way in which we can surely find remission of sins, and in the Word we are sure to find this remission. If we seek it not there, our sins will be retained, do what we may; for . . . there is no remission except in the Word of Christ. This Word, however, has been entrusted to the apostles and all Christians, and they are to apply it; he who seeks any other remedy for the ills of sin, shall not find it, no matter what he may do to accomplish that end."[66]

Then having established that principle, that forgiveness is alone in the Word, Luther sends the sinner to the

---

[66]House Postil. *Am Sonntag Quasi modo geniti.* W. LII, 273f. Tr. by Saarnivaara, *Op. cit.,* p. 34. Within the framework of the "Word" in Luther are always included Baptism and the Supper as Means of Grace.

Church to receive it. "Whoever now desires remission of sins, let him go to his minister or to some other fellow Christian who has God's Word, and he will surely find consolation there."[67]

How is the sinner to receive this word of forgiveness from the Church? The answer, as we would expect from Luther, is faith. And when the sinner comes to the minister convicted and fearful, he is to direct him to the Word which he declares to him. If he cannot believe he is worthy of forgiveness, he must still believe the Word of God, for He does not lie. "Although I cannot give you the Holy Ghost and faith, I can yet declare them unto you; if you believe, you have it."[68] And this Word which the minister declares is the very means by which the Holy Spirit quickens that vacillating faith of the sinner.

Here again Luther firmly plants that pillar of the Reformation, the doctrine of the Means of Grace, which has become so distinctive of Lutheranism. "God has ordained that no one shall come to the knowledge of Christ, nor obtain the forgiveness acquired by Him, nor receive the Holy Ghost, without the use of external and public means; but God has embraced this treasure in the oral word or public ministry, and will not perform His work in a corner or mysteriously in the heart, but will have it heralded and distributed openly among the people. . . . Therefore this part also, namely, the external word or preaching, belongs to Christianity as a channel or means through which we attain unto the forgiveness of sins, or the righteousness of Christ, with which Christ reveals and offers us His grace or lays it into our bosom, and without

---
[67] *Loc. cit.*
[68] *Am. XII. Sonntag nach Trinitatis* . . . W. XXII, 224. Lenker XIV, 209.

which no one would ever come to a knowledge of this treasure. . . . Therefore I have always taught that the oral word must precede everything else, must be comprehended with the ear, if the Holy Ghost is to enter the heart, who through the Word enlightens it and works faith. Consequently, faith does not come except through the hearing and oral preaching of the Gospel, in which it has its beginning, growth and strength."[69]

At this point Luther lays down one more principle which is vital to the right understanding and use of absolution. The confessing sinner must not be made to think that his forgiveness depends on the degree of his contrition. And the minister must therefore beware lest he offer the sinner a conditional forgiveness or absolution. "Uncertain absolution is the same as no absolution; yea, it is perfectly the same as lie and deceit. . . . But it must be uncertain [the Roman Catholics hold] since repentance whereon it depends is uncertain; for who is able to say that his repentance is sufficient before God? And what repentance can be sufficient before God? For our own repentance does not suffice in His sight, but Christ Himself with His suffering must be our repentance and satisfaction before God. . . . Keep in your mind that the Key or forgiveness of sins is not founded on our contrition or worthiness . . . , but to the contrary, we should base our contrition, work, heart, everything, on the Key and rely on it with our whole conviction, as on God's Word. . . . It is true, you should repent and be contrite; but the assumption that forgiveness of sins would become sure and the operation of the Key confirmed by that, would mean giving up faith and denying Christ. He will not

---
[69]*Church Postil, 19th Sunday after Trinity, Gospel Sermon.* Lenker 14, 224.

grant and impart you the forgiveness of sins through the Key for your own sake, but for His own sake, by sheer mercy."[70]

Luther is speaking from deep experience here, sometimes bitter, as well as from the Word itself. And we can see behind this language the answer to the abuses he saw on both sides of him. He remembered how penances and works of all kinds had been demanded of him before he could be sure of forgiveness. He saw on the other side of him the subjective emphasis of the sectarians, who had no grasp of the objective Means of Grace. And he warns them both, "If a man were required to say he is truly penitent, he would be driven to presumption and to the impossible task of knowing all his sins and evil.... Christians ought to be instructed that every penitent (one who makes a confession and seeks absolution) may know that before God no contrition is worthy or sufficient, and may say, 'Behold, dear Lord, I know that I will not be found truly contrite before Thy judgment, and that there is still much evil lust in me which hinders true contrition, yet, because Thou hast promised grace, I flee from Thy judgment, and . . . put my reliance in this sacrament (absolution).' If the minister inquires about his contrition, he ought to say, 'Sir, in my own eyes I am contrite, but in God's sight it is but a poor contrition with which I am not able to stand in His presence; yet I hope in His grace, which you are now, at His Command, to promise me.' "[71]

When Luther thus speaks about assurance, he does not lead the sinner out on the thin ice of inner experience.

---
[70] *Von den Schlüsseln.* W. XXX, pt. 2, 480f.; 496. Tr. by Saarnivaara. *Op. cit.,* p.. 43f.
[71] *Grund und Ursach.* W. VII, 384. Tr. by Saarnivaara. *Op. cit.,* p. 44f.

He gives him the sure Word and bids him trust in that, and that alone. And the minister must show the same trust in the Word when he offers it to the sinner, lest he disturb and confuse him. "When a Christian hears and is made to believe that the Key can err and go amiss, he can then by no means rely and believe that which the Key promises him. For of that in which one believes one must be sure and absolutely convinced beyond any doubt that it is God's Word and truth. Otherwise there can be born only uncertain assumption and wavering faith, and even unbelief. ... We are not speaking now on the question who believes and who does not believe, for we do know very well that only few believe, but we speak of what the Keys accomplish and give. Many people do not believe the Gospel, but the Gospel, nevertheless, does not lie. A certain king gives you a castle: if you do not accept it, the king has yet not lied nor deceived, but you have deceived yourself, and the fault is yours; the king has surely given it."[72]

The importance of finding our assurance in the Word and not in our feeling of contrition comes out beautifully in one of Luther's "Table Talks," "The forgiveness of sins is declared only in God's Word, and there we must seek it; for it is grounded on God's promises. God forgives thy sins, not because thou feelest them and art sorry, but He forgives thy sins because He is merciful, and because He has promised to forgive for Christ's sake."[73]

---
[72] *Von den Schlüsseln.* W. XXX, pt. 2, 480-483, 499. Tr. by Saarnivaara. *Op. cit.,* p. 45f.
[73] *The Table Talk of Martin Luther. Op. cit.,* p. 139.

CONCLUSION

"I believe in the holy Christian Church, the Communion of Saints, the forgiveness of sins." Luther's faith is radiant with a profound catholicity when he contemplates this great article of the Apostles' Creed. He can think of neither faith nor personal experience of forgiveness outside of the Church. "I believe that in this congregation, and nowhere else, there is forgiveness of sins; that outside of it, good works, however great they be or many, are of no avail for the forgiveness of sins; but that within it, no matter how much, how greatly or how often men may sin, nothing can hinder forgiveness of sins, which abides wherever and as long as this one congregation abides."[74]

This is indeed the meaning of the Body of Christ. It is as a member of this Body that I can say in faith, "I am crucified with Christ: nevertheless I live; yet not I, but Christ liveth in me." The Church, too, can make the same confession. For in the Church Christ lives, and through the Church He carries on His saving mission in the world and to the world. The members of the Body of Christ were never meant to sit behind stone walls with folded hands, letting the world go to the devil. As L. S. Thornton says so well, "The life common to Christ and His Church does not exist for its own sake. It has a mediatorial character. The Messiah and His people are sent from God to the world. . . . Thus the Church lives one life with the incarnate Son; and in that life, so shared, His mission to the world is fulfilled."[75]

---

[74] *A Brief Explanation of the Ten Commandments, the Creed, and the Lord's Prayer,* 1520. Holman, II. 373.
[75] L. S. Thornton, *The Common Life in the Body of Christ,* p. 444. Westminster: Dacre Press, 1944.

The forgiveness of sins in the life of the Church, as of the individual, is at the heart of our faith, but also at the heart of our life. And Luther, in the name of Christ, sends the Church out into the stream of life to live and radiate the forgiven life in the world of sinners. He has no patience with the quietism of much of the Church which bears his name today. Of a similar situation in Wittenberg he says, "I notice that you have a great deal to say of the doctrine which is preached to you, of faith and of love. This is not surprising; an ass can almost intone the lessons, and why should you not be able to repeat the doctrines and formulas? Dear friends, the kingdom of God—and we are that kingdom—consists not in speech or in words, but in deeds, in works and exercises. God does not want hearers and repeaters of words, but doers and followers who exercise themselves in the faith that worketh by love. For a faith without love is not enough—rather it is not faith at all, but a counterfeit of faith, just as a face seen in a mirror is not a real face but merely the reflection of a face."

At the Cross of Christ faith and love are born in the individual heart. But at the same moment of birth the believer is planted in the Church, grafted into the Body of Christ. There he lives his faith, not in selfish loneliness, but in the loving fellowship of other believers, in the Communion of Saints. This is the Body of Christ. This is the Light of the world! Word and Sacrament kindled it. Word and Sacrament still keep it burning.

Luther and the Reformation under God restored again the beauty of the Church. Sweeping away the man-made instruments of tyranny—hierarchy, Papacy, penances and all the rest—he released the people from a religion of fear, and through the Gospel of grace alone he ushered them into the glorious liberty of the children of God. The beauty of the Church has probably never been painted in more colorful words than in those of the great Reformer in one of his "Table Talks." "The amaranth is a flower that grows in August: it is more a stalk than a flower, is easily broken off, and grows in joyful and pleasant sort; when all other flowers are gone and decayed, then this, being sprinkled with water, becomes fair and green again; so that in winter they use it to make garlands thereof. It is called amaranth from this, that it neither withers nor decays.

"I know nothing more like unto the church than this flower, the amaranth. For although the church bathes her garment in the blood of the Lamb, and is colored over with red, yet she is more fair, comely, and beautiful than any state and assembly upon the face of the earth. She alone is embraced and beloved of the Son of God, as His sweet and amiable spouse, in whom only He takes joy and delight, and whereon His heart alone depends; He utterly rejects and loathes others, that contemn or falsify His Gospel.

"Moreover, the church willingly suffers herself to be plucked and broken off, that is, she is loving, patient, and obedient to Christ her bridegroom in the cross; she grows and increases again, fair, joyful, and pleasant, that is, she gains the greatest fruit and profit thereby; she learns to know God aright, to call upon Him freely and undauntedly, to confess His word and doctrine, and produces many fair and glorious virtues.

"At last, the body and stalk remain whole and sound, and cannot be rooted out, although raging and swelling be made against some of the members, and these be torn away. For like as the amaranth never withers or decays, even so the church can never be destroyed or rooted out. But what is most wonderful, the amaranth has this quality, that when it is sprinkled with water, and dipped therein, it becomes fresh and green again, as if it were raised and wakened from the dead. Even so likewise the church will by God be raised and wakened out of the grave, and become living again; will everlastingly praise, extol, and laud the Father of our Lord and Savior Jesus Christ, His Son and our Redeemer, together with the Holy Ghost. For though temporal empires, kingdoms, and principalities have their changings, and like flowers soon fall and fade away, this kingdom, which is so deep-rooted, by no power can be destroyed or wasted, but remains eternally."[76]

Shall we ever learn how important it is for us to become conscious of the *inner unity* of the Church in the one faith in Christ? It is true, outward unity would be the ideal which would show the world this unity of faith. But how confused we become when we begin thinking in terms of a visible organization. The outward form is human and will always be imperfect. Pride and error will separate us, even as Christians. Some groups will drift into a sectarian attitude, exalting some error which taints their whole faith, causing schism and conflict. Others will be so overcome by one truth that they will forget the *whole* truth.

And so the Christian must never hope to experience fully the *oneness* of the Church in the Body of Christ through any outward arrangement made by men. He

---
[76]*The Table Talk of Martin Luther. Op cit.*, p. 172.

finds the Body of Christ not identified with some particular outward organization. He finds it where the one Gospel is preached, where men worship the one God-Man, where men are baptized into the Kingdom and kept through the real Body and Blood of Christ according to His institution and promise. He deplores the divisions in the outward life of Christians. Yet he can still see through names and denominations and sects and be conscious that throughout the world where men gather about His Word and Sacrament there are his brothers and sisters in the faith. And when out of Europe or Asia, Africa or the Americas comes the word that men are dying for their faith in Christ, dying because they put the Word of God above the word of men and of states, he knows that there are his kinfolk in the Spirit, his fellow-members in the Body of Christ. The Communion of Saints, in which both are bound to Christ, binds them together in the bonds of a great faith and a deep love. He knows that throughout the world are brothers in the faith confessing with him every Lord's Day, "I believe in God the Father. . . . And in Jesus Christ, His only Son, our Lord. . . . I believe in the Holy Ghost." And in that faith they are together lifted up above the divisions, the denominations, the destroyed churches, to confess together a sublime reality and glorious experience, "I believe in the holy Christian Church, the Communion of Saints." "And I believe in one holy catholic and apostolic Church. I acknowledge one Baptism for the remission of sins; and I look for the resurrection of the dead, and the life of the world to come. Amen."

www.ingramcontent.com/pod-product-compliance
Lightning Source LLC
Chambersburg PA
CBHW051059160426
43193CB00010B/1242